CW01308242

The Ultimate UK Air

Recipes For Beginners

Super-Crispy and Affordable Homemade

Air Fryer Cookbook

Linda B. Renteria

All Rights Reserved.

The contents of this book may not be reproduced, copied or transmitted without the direct written permission of the author or publisher. Under no circumstances will the publisher or the author be held responsible or liable for any damage, compensation or pecuniary loss arising directly or indirectly from the information contained in this book.

Legal notice. This book is protected by copyright. It is intended for personal use only. You may not modify, distribute, sell, use, quote or paraphrase any part or content of this book without the consent of the author or publisher.

Notice Of Disclaimer.

Please note that the information in this document is intended for educational and entertainment purposes only. Every effort has been made to provide accurate, up-to-date, reliable and complete information. No warranty of any kind is declared or implied. The reader acknowledges that the author does not engage in the provision of legal, financial, medical or professional advice. The content in this book has been obtained from a variety of sources. Please consult a licensed professional before attempting any of the techniques described in this book. By reading this document, the reader agrees that in no event shall the author be liable for any direct or indirect damages, including but not limited to errors, omissions or inaccuracies, resulting from the use of the information in this document.

CONTENTS

Breakfast & Snacks And Fries Recipes 11

Halloumi Fries 11

Patatas Bravas 11

Plantain Fries 12

Healthy Stuffed Peppers 12

Blanket Breakfast Eggs 13

French Toast 13

Tangy Breakfast Hash 14

Cumin Shoestring Carrots 14

Raspberry Breakfast Pockets 15

Potato Fries 15

Your Favourite Breakfast Bacon 16

Easy Cheesy Scrambled Eggs 16

Breakfast Doughnuts 17

Easy Air Fryer Sausage 17

Hard Boiled Eggs Air Fryer Style 18

Courgette Fries 18

Oozing Baked Eggs 19

Cheese Scones 19

Breakfast "pop Tarts" 20

Healthy Breakfast Bagels 20

Baba Ganoush 21

Apple Crisps 21

Vegetarian & Vegan Recipes 22

Veggie Lasagne 22

Veggie Bakes 22
Broccoli Cheese 23
Baked Aubergine Slices With Yogurt Dressing 23
Whole Wheat Pizza 24
Quinoa-stuffed Romano Peppers 24
Goat's Cheese Tartlets 25
Air Fryer Cheese Sandwich 25
Mini Quiche 26
Spinach And Feta Croissants 26
Butternut Squash Falafel 27
Sticky Tofu With Cauliflower Rice 27
Sweet Potato Taquitos 28
Ravioli Air Fryer Style 28
Shakshuka 29
Bbq Soy Curls 29
Gnocchi Caprese 30
Miso Mushrooms On Sourdough Toast 30
Tofu Bowls 31
Cheese, Tomato & Pesto Crustless Quiches 31
Courgette Meatballs 32
Tempura Veggies 32
Sauces & Snack And Appetiser Recipes 33
Bacon Smokies 33
Garlic Cheese Bread 33
Korean Chicken Wings 34
Waffle Fries 34

Pretzel Bites 35
Onion Pakoda 35
Chicken & Bacon Parcels 36
Garlic Pizza Toast 36
Jalapeño Poppers 37
Mozzarella Sticks 37
Tasty Pumpkin Seeds 38
Salt And Vinegar Chips 38
Mac & Cheese Bites 39
Pepperoni Bread 39
Onion Bahji 40
Tortellini Bites 40
Popcorn Tofu 41
Corn Nuts 41
Italian Rice Balls 42
Spicy Peanuts 42
Cheese Wontons 43
Scotch Eggs 43

Fish & Seafood Recipes 44

Pesto Salmon 44
Coconut Shrimp 44
Tilapia Fillets 45
Fish Taco Cauliflower Rice Bowls 45
Shrimp Wrapped With Bacon 46
Shrimp With Yum Yum Sauce 46
Fish Sticks With Tartar Sauce Batter 47

Crunchy Fish 47
Crispy Nacho Prawns 48
Fish In Parchment Paper 48
Baked Panko Cod 49
Parmesan-coated Fish Fingers 49
Gluten Free Honey And Garlic Shrimp 50
Tandoori Salmon 50
Garlic-parsley Prawns 51
Store-cupboard Fishcakes 51
Thai-style Tuna Fishcakes 52
Mahi Fish Tacos 53
Traditional Fish And Chips 53
Peppery Lemon Shrimp 54
Thai Salmon Patties 54
Lemon Pepper Shrimp 55
Beef & Lamb And Pork Recipes 55
Mongolian Beef 55
Asian Meatballs 56
Beef Kebobs 56
Traditional Empanadas 57
Salt And Pepper Belly Pork 57
Japanese Pork Chops 58
Lamb Calzone 58
Fillet Mignon Wrapped In Bacon 59
Hamburgers With Feta 59
Sausage Burritos 60

Tahini Beef Bites 60
Taco Lasagne Pie 61
Meatballs In Tomato Sauce 61
Steak And Mushrooms 62
Pork Belly With Crackling 62
Roast Pork 63
Chinese Pork With Pineapple 63
Char Siu Buffalo 64
Pork Chops With Raspberry And Balsamic 64
Pork Chilli Cheese Dogs 65
Chinese Chilli Beef 65
Beef Bulgogi Burgers 66
Poultry Recipes 66
Bbq Chicken Tenders 66
Honey Cajun Chicken Thighs 67
Chicken Fried Rice 67
Chicken Tikka 68
Whole Chicken 68
Healthy Bang Bang Chicken 69
Charred Chicken Breasts 69
Air Fried Maple Chicken Thighs 70
Grain-free Chicken Katsu 71
Chicken And Cheese Chimichangas 72
Turkey Cutlets In Mushroom Sauce 72
Quick Chicken Nuggets 73
Thai Turkey Burgers 73

Olive Stained Turkey Breast 74
Chicken Fajitas 74
Hawaiian Chicken 75
Air Fryer Bbq Chicken 75
Chicken Parmesan With Marinara Sauce 76
Cheddar & Bbq Stuffed Chicken 76
Buffalo Wings 77
Buttermilk Chicken 77
Pizza Chicken Nuggets 78

Side Dishes Recipes 78

Butternut Squash 78
Homemade Croquettes 79
Tex Mex Hash Browns 79
Orange Sesame Cauliflower 80
Crispy Broccoli 80
Courgette Gratin 81
Cauliflower With Hot Sauce And Blue Cheese Sauce 81
Aubergine Parmesan 82
Roasted Okra 82
Asparagus Spears 83
Alternative Stuffed Potatoes 83
Potato Wedges With Rosemary 84
Asparagus Fries 84
Mediterranean Vegetables 85
Onion Rings 85
Garlic And Parsley Potatoes 86

Egg Fried Rice 86

Sweet And Sticky Parsnips And Carrots 87

Super Easy Fries 87

Zingy Brussels Sprouts 88

Hasselback New Potatoes 88

Yorkshire Puddings 89

Desserts Recipes 89

Brownies 89

Chocolate And Berry Pop Tarts 90

White Chocolate Pudding 91

Cinnamon Bites 91

Chocolate Eclairs 92

Chocolate Souffle 92

Banana Bread 93

Cherry Pies 93

Apple Crumble 94

Peach Pies(2) 94

Pop Tarts 95

Lemon Tarts 95

Thai Fried Bananas 96

Peanut Butter & Chocolate Baked Oats 96

Pumpkin Spiced Bread Pudding 97

Apple Chips With Yogurt Dip 97

Chocolate Cake 98

Peach Pies(1) 98

Coffee, Chocolate Chip, And Banana Bread 99

Chocolate Orange Muffins 100

Chocolate Shortbread Balls 100

Sweet Potato Dessert Fries 101

RECIPES INDEX 102

Breakfast & Snacks And Fries Recipes

Halloumi Fries

Servings: 2
Cooking Time:xx
Ingredients:

- 225 g/8 oz. halloumi
- 40 g/heaped ¼ cup plain/all-purpose flour (gluten-free if you wish)
- ½ teaspoon sweet smoked paprika
- ½ teaspoon dried oregano
- ¼ teaspoon mild chilli/chili powder
- olive oil or avocado oil, for spraying

Directions:

1. Preheat the air-fryer to 180°C/350°F.
2. Slice the halloumi into fries roughly 2 x 1.5 cm/¾ x ⅝ in.
3. Mix the flour and seasoning in a bowl and dip each halloumi stick into the flour to coat. Spray with a little oil.
4. Add the fries to the preheated air-fryer and air-fry for 5 minutes. Serve immediately.

Patatas Bravas

Servings: 4
Cooking Time:xx
Ingredients:

- 300g potatoes
- 1 tsp garlic powder
- 1 tbsp avocado oil
- 1 tbsp smoked paprika
- Salt and pepper to taste

Directions:

1. Peel the potatoes and cut them into cubes
2. Bring a large saucepan of water to the boil and add the potatoes, cooking for 6 minutes
3. Strain the potatoes and place them on a piece of kitchen towel, allowing to dry
4. Take a large mixing bowl and add the garlic powder, salt, and pepper and add the avocado oil, mixing together well
5. Add the potatoes to the bowl and coat liberally
6. Place the potatoes into the basket and arrange them with space in-between
7. Set your fryer to 200°C
8. Cook the potatoes for 15 minutes, giving them a shake at the halfway point
9. Remove and serve

Plantain Fries

Servings: 2
Cooking Time:xx
Ingredients:

- 1 ripe plantain (yellow and brown outside skin)
- 1 teaspoon olive oil
- ¼ teaspoon salt

Directions:

1. Preheat the air-fryer to 180°C/350°F.
2. Peel the plantain and slice into fries about 6 x 1 cm/2½ x ½ in. Toss the fries in oil and salt, making sure every fry is coated.
3. Tip into the preheated air-fryer in a single layer (you may need to cook them in two batches, depending on the size of your air-fryer) and air-fry for 13–14 minutes until brown on the outside and soft on the inside. Serve immediately.

Healthy Stuffed Peppers

Servings: 2
Cooking Time:xx
Ingredients:

- 1 large bell pepper, deseeded and cut into halves
- 1 tsp olive oil
- 4 large eggs
- Salt and pepper to taste

Directions:

1. Take your peppers and rub a little olive oil on the edges
2. Into each pepper, crack one egg and season with salt and pepper
3. You will need to insert a trivet into your air fryer to hold the peppers, and then arrange the peppers evenly
4. Set your fryer to 200°C and cook for 13 minutes
5. Once cooked, remove and serve with a little more seasoning, if required

Blanket Breakfast Eggs

Servings: 2
Cooking Time:xx
Ingredients:

- 2 eggs
- 2 slices of sandwich bread
- Olive oil spray
- Salt and pepper to taste

Directions:

1. Preheat your air fryer to 190°C and spray with a little oil
2. Meanwhile, take your bread and cut a hole into the middle of each piece
3. Place one slice inside your fryer and crack one egg into the middle
4. Season with a little salt and pepper
5. Cook for 5 minutes, before turning over and cooking for a further 2 minutes
6. Remove the first slice and repeat the process with the remaining slice of bread and egg

French Toast

Servings: 2
Cooking Time:xx
Ingredients:

- 2 beaten eggs
- 2 tbsp softened butter
- 4 slices of sandwich bread
- 1 tsp cinnamon
- 1 tsp nutmeg
- 1 tsp ground cloves
- 1 tsp maple syrup

Directions:

1. Preheat your fryer to 180°C
2. Take a bowl and add the eggs, salt, cinnamon, nutmeg, and cloves, combining well
3. Take your bread and butter each side, cutting into strips
4. Dip the bread slices into the egg mixture
5. Arrange each slice into the basket of your fryer
6. Cook for 2 minutes
7. Take the basket out and spray with a little cooking spray
8. Turn over the slices and place back into the fryer
9. Cook for 4 minutes
10. Remove and serve with maple syrup

Tangy Breakfast Hash

Servings: 6
Cooking Time:xx

Ingredients:

- 2 tbsp olive oil
- 2 sweet potatoes, cut into cubes
- 1 tbsp smoked paprika
- 1 tsp salt
- 1 tsp black pepper
- 2 slices of bacon, cut into small pieces

Directions:

1. Preheat your air fryer to 200°C
2. Pour the olive oil into a large mixing bowl
3. Add the bacon, seasonings, potatoes and toss to evenly coat
4. Transfer the mixture into the air fryer and cook for 12-16 minutes
5. Stir after 10 minutes and continue to stir periodically for another 5 minutes

Cumin Shoestring Carrots

Servings: 2
Cooking Time:xx

Ingredients:

- 300 g/10½ oz. carrots
- 1 teaspoon cornflour/cornstarch
- 1 teaspoon ground cumin
- ¼ teaspoon salt
- 1 tablespoon olive oil
- garlic mayonnaise, to serve

Directions:

1. Preheat the air-fryer to 200°C/400°F.
2. Peel the carrots and cut into thin fries, roughly 10 cm x 1 cm x 5 mm/4 x ½ x ¼ in. Toss the carrots in a bowl with all the other ingredients.
3. Add the carrots to the preheated air-fryer and air-fry for 9 minutes, shaking the drawer of the air-fryer a couple of times during cooking. Serve with garlic mayo on the side.

Raspberry Breakfast Pockets

Servings: 1
Cooking Time:xx
Ingredients:

- 2 slices of sandwich bread
- 1 tbsp soft cream cheese
- 1 tbsp raspberry jam
- 1 tbsp milk
- 1 egg

Directions:

1. Take one slice of the bread and add one tablespoon of jam into the middle
2. Take the second slice and add the cream cheese into the middle
3. Using a blunt knife, spread the jam and the cheese across the bread, but don't go to the outer edges
4. Take a small bowl and whisk the eggs and the milk together
5. Set your fryer to 190°C and spray with a little oil
6. Dip your sandwich into the egg and arrange inside your fryer
7. Cook for 5 minutes on the first side, turn and cook for another 2 minutes

Potato Fries

Servings: 2
Cooking Time:xx
Ingredients:

- 2 large potatoes (baking potato size)
- 1 teaspoon olive oil
- salt

Directions:

1. Peel the potatoes and slice into fries about 5 x 1.5cm/¾ x ¾ in. by the length of the potato. Submerge the fries in a bowl of cold water and place in the fridge for about 10 minutes.
2. Meanwhile, preheat the air-fryer to 160°C/325°F.
3. Drain the fries thoroughly, then toss in the oil and season. Tip into the preheated air-fryer in a single layer (you may need to cook them in two batches, depending on the size of your air-fryer). Air-fry for 15 minutes, tossing once during cooking by shaking the air-fryer drawer, then increase the temperature of the air-fryer to 200°C/400°F and cook for a further 3 minutes. Serve immediately.

Your Favourite Breakfast Bacon

Servings: 2
Cooking Time:xx
Ingredients:

- 4-5 rashers of lean bacon, fat cut off
- Salt and pepper for seasoning

Directions:

1. Line your air fryer basket with parchment paper
2. Place the bacon in the basket
3. Set the fryer to 200°C
4. Cook for 10 minutes for crispy. If you want it very crispy, cook for another 2 minutes

Easy Cheesy Scrambled Eggs

Servings: 1
Cooking Time:xx
Ingredients:

- 1 tbsp butter
- 2 eggs
- 100g grated cheese
- 2 tbsp milk
- Salt and pepper for seasoning

Directions:

1. Add the butter inside the air fryer pan and cook at 220°C until the butter has melted
2. Add the eggs and milk to a bowl and combine, seasoning to your liking
3. Pour the eggs into the butter panned cook for 3 minutes, stirring around lightly to scramble
4. Add the cheese and cook for another 2 more minutes

Breakfast Doughnuts

Servings: 4
Cooking Time:xx
Ingredients:

- 1 packet of Pillsbury Grands
- 5 tbsp raspberry jam
- 1 tbsp melted butter
- 5 tbsp sugar

Directions:

1. Preheat your air fryer to 250°C
2. Place the Pillsbury Grands into the air fryer and cook for around 5m minutes
3. Remove and place to one side
4. Take a large bowl and add the sugar
5. Coat the doughnuts in the melted butter, coating evenly
6. Dip into the sugar and coat evenly once more
7. Using an icing bag, add the jam into the bag and pipe an even amount into each doughnut
8. Eat warm or cold

Easy Air Fryer Sausage

Servings: 5
Cooking Time:xx
Ingredients:

- 5 uncooked sausages
- 1 tbsp mustard
- Salt and pepper for seasoning

Directions:

1. Line the basket of your fryer with parchment paper
2. Arrange the sausages inside the basket
3. Set to 180°C and cook for 15 minutes
4. Turn the sausages over and cook for another 5 minutes
5. Remove and cool
6. Drizzle the mustard over the top and season to your liking

Hard Boiled Eggs Air Fryer Style

Servings: 2
Cooking Time:xx
Ingredients:

- 4 large eggs
- 1 tsp cayenne pepper
- Salt and pepper for seasoning

Directions:

1. Preheat the air fryer to 220°C
2. Take a wire rack and place inside the air fryer
3. Lay the eggs on the rack
4. Cook for between 15-17 minutes, depending upon how you like your eggs
5. Remove from the fryer and place in a bowl of cold water for around 5 minutes
6. Peel and season with the cayenne and the salt and pepper

Courgette Fries

Servings: 2
Cooking Time:xx
Ingredients:

- 1 courgette/zucchini
- 3 tablespoons plain/all-purpose flour (gluten-free if you wish)
- 1/4 teaspoon salt
- 1/4 teaspoon freshly ground black pepper
- 60 g/3/4 cup dried breadcrumbs (gluten-free if you wish; see page 9)
- 1 teaspoon dried oregano
- 20 g/1/4 cup finely grated Parmesan
- 1 egg, beaten

Directions:

1. Preheat the air-fryer to 180°C/350°F.
2. Slice the courgette/zucchini into fries about 1.5 x 1.5 x 5 cm/5/8 x 5/8 x 2 in.
3. Season the flour with salt and pepper. Combine the breadcrumbs with the oregano and Parmesan.
4. Dip the courgettes/zucchini in the flour (shaking off any excess flour), then the egg, then the seasoned breadcrumbs.
5. Add the fries to the preheated air-fryer and air-fry for 15 minutes. They should be crispy on the outside but soft on the inside. Serve immediately.

Oozing Baked Eggs

Servings: 2
Cooking Time:xx
Ingredients:

- 4 eggs
- 140g smoked gouda cheese, cut into small pieces
- Salt and pepper to taste

Directions:

1. You will need two ramekin dishes and spray each one before using
2. Crack two eggs into each ramekin dish
3. Add half of the Gouda cheese to each dish
4. Season and place into the air fryer
5. Cook at 350°C for 15 minutes, until the eggs are cooked as you like them

Cheese Scones

Servings:12
Cooking Time:xx
Ingredients:

- ½ teaspoon baking powder
- 210 g/1½ cups self-raising/self-rising flour (gluten-free if you wish), plus extra for dusting
- 50 g/3½ tablespoons cold butter, cubed
- 125 g/1½ cups grated mature Cheddar
- a pinch of cayenne pepper
- a pinch of salt
- 100 ml/7 tablespoons milk, plus extra for brushing the tops of the scones

Directions:

1. Mix the baking powder with the flour in a bowl, then add the butter and rub into the flour to form a crumblike texture. Add the cheese, cayenne pepper and salt and stir. Then add the milk, a little at a time, and bring together into a ball of dough.
2. Dust your work surface with flour. Roll the dough flat until about 1.5 cm/⅝ in. thick. Cut out the scones using a 6-cm/2½-in. diameter cookie cutter. Gather the offcuts into a ball, re-roll and cut more scones – you should get about 12 scones from the mixture. Place the scones on an air-fryer liner or a piece of pierced parchment paper.
3. Preheat the air-fryer to 180°C/350°F.
4. Add the scones to the preheated air-fryer and air-fry for 8 minutes, turning them over halfway to cook the other side. Remove and allow to cool a little, then serve warm.

Breakfast "pop Tarts"

Servings: 6
Cooking Time:xx
Ingredients:

- 2 slices of prepared pie crust, shortbread or filo will work fine
- 2 tbsp strawberry jam
- 60ml plain yogurt
- 1 tsp cornstarch
- 1 tsp Stevia sweetener
- 2 tbsp cream cheese
- A drizzle of olive oil

Directions:

1. Lay your pie crust flat and cut into 6 separate rectangular pieces
2. In a small bowl, mix together the cornstarch and the jam
3. Spread 1 tablespoon of the mixture on top of the crust
4. Fold each crust over to form the tart
5. Seal down the edges using a fork
6. Arrange your tarts inside the frying basket and spray with a little olive oil
7. Heat to 175°C and cook for 10 minutes
8. Meanwhile, combine the yogurt, cream cheese and Stevia in a bowl
9. Remove the tarts and allow to cool
10. Once cool, add the frosting on top and sprinkle with the sugar sprinkles

Healthy Breakfast Bagels

Servings: 2
Cooking Time:xx
Ingredients:

- 170g self raising flour
- 120ml plain yogurt
- 1 egg

Directions:

1. Take a large mixing bowl, combine the flour and the yogurt to create a dough
2. Cover a flat surface with a little extra flour and set the dough down
3. Create four separate and even balls
4. Roll each ball out into a rope shape and form a bagel with each
5. Take a small mixing bowl and whisk the egg
6. Brush the egg over the top of the bagel
7. Arrange the bagels inside your fryer evenly
8. Cook at 170°C for 10 minutes
9. Allow to cool before serving

Baba Ganoush

Servings: 4
Cooking Time:xx

Ingredients:

- 1 large aubergine/eggplant, sliced in half lengthways
- ½ teaspoon salt
- 5 tablespoons olive oil
- 1 bulb garlic
- 30 g/2 tablespoons tahini or nut butter
- 2 tablespoons freshly squeezed lemon juice
- ½ teaspoon ground cumin
- ¼ teaspoon smoked paprika
- salt and freshly ground black pepper
- 3 tablespoons freshly chopped flat-leaf parsley

Directions:

1. Preheat the air-fryer to 200°C/400°F.
2. Lay the aubergine/eggplant halves cut side up. Sprinkle over the salt, then drizzle over 1 tablespoon of oil. Cut the top off the garlic bulb, brush the exposed cloves with a little olive oil, then wrap in foil. Place the aubergine/eggplant and foil-wrapped garlic in the preheated air-fryer and air-fry for 15–20 minutes until the inside of the aubergine is soft and buttery in texture.
3. Scoop the flesh of the aubergine into a bowl. Squeeze out about 1 tablespoon of the cooked garlic and add to the bowl with the remaining 4 tablespoons of olive oil, the tahini/nut butter, lemon juice, spices and salt and pepper to taste. Mix well and serve with fresh flat-leaf parsley sprinkled over.

Apple Crisps

Servings: 2
Cooking Time:xx

Ingredients:

- 2 apples, chopped
- 1 tsp cinnamon
- 2 tbsp brown sugar
- 1 tsp lemon juice
- 2.5 tbsp plain flour
- 3 tbsp oats
- 2 tbsp cold butter
- Pinch of salt

Directions:

1. Preheat the air fryer to 260°C
2. Take a 5" baking dish and crease
3. Take a large bowl and combine the apples with the sugar, cinnamon and lemon juice
4. Add the mixture to the baking dish and cover with aluminium foil
5. Place in the air fryer and cook for 15 minutes
6. Open the lid and cook for another 5 minutes
7. Combine the rest of the ingredients in a food processor, until a crumble-type mixture occurs
8. Add over the top of the cooked apples
9. Cook with the lid open for another 5 minutes
10. Allow to cool a little before serving

Vegetarian & Vegan Recipes

Veggie Lasagne

Servings: 1
Cooking Time:xx
Ingredients:

- 2 lasagne sheets
- Pinch of salt
- 100g pasta sauce
- 50g ricotta
- 60g chopped basil
- 40g chopped spinach
- 3 tbsp grated courgette

Directions:

1. Break the lasagne sheets in half, bring a pan of water to boil
2. Cook the lasagne sheets for about 8 minutes, drain and pat dry
3. Add 2 tbsp of pasta sauce to a mini loaf tin
4. Add a lasagne sheet, top with ricotta, basil and spinach, then add courgette
5. Place another lasagne sheet on top
6. Add a couple of tbsp pasta sauce, basil, spinach and courgette
7. Add the last lasagne sheet, top with pasta sauce and ricotta
8. Cover with foil and place in the air fryer
9. Cook at 180°C for 10 mins, remove foil and cook for another 3 minutes

Veggie Bakes

Servings: 2
Cooking Time:xx
Ingredients:

- Any type of leftover vegetable bake you have
- 30g flour

Directions:

1. Preheat the air fryer to 180°C
2. Mix the flour with the leftover vegetable bake
3. Shape into balls and place in the air fryer
4. Cook for 10 minutes

Broccoli Cheese

Servings: 2
Cooking Time:xx

Ingredients:

- 250g broccoli
- Cooking spray
- 10 tbsp evaporated milk
- 300g Mexican cheese
- 4 tsp Amarillo paste
- 6 saltine crackers

Directions:

1. Heat the air fryer to 190°C
2. Place the broccoli in the air fryer spray with cooking oil and cook for about 6 minutes
3. Place the remaining ingredients in a blender and process until smooth
4. Place in a bowl and microwave for 30 seconds
5. Pour over the broccoli and serve

Baked Aubergine Slices With Yogurt Dressing

Servings: 2
Cooking Time:xx

Ingredients:

- 1 aubergine/eggplant, sliced 1.5 cm/⅝ in. thick
- 3 tablespoons olive oil
- ½ teaspoon salt
- YOGURT DRESSING
- 1 small garlic clove
- 1 tablespoon tahini or nut butter
- 100 g/½ cup Greek yogurt
- 2 teaspoons freshly squeezed lemon juice
- 1 tablespoon runny honey
- a pinch of salt
- a pinch of ground cumin
- a pinch of sumac
- TO SERVE
- 30 g/1 oz. rocket/arugula
- 2 tablespoons freshly chopped mint
- 3 tablespoons pomegranate seeds

Directions:

1. Preheat the air-fryer to 180°C/350°F.
2. Drizzle the olive oil over each side of the aubergine/eggplant slices. Sprinkle with salt. Add the aubergines to the preheated air-fryer and air-fry for 10 minutes, turning halfway through cooking.
3. Meanwhile, make the dressing by combining all the ingredients in a mini food processor (alterantively, finely chop the garlic, add to a jar with the other ingredients and shake vigorously).
4. Serve the cooked aubergine slices on a bed of rocket/arugula, drizzled with the dressing and with the mint and pomegranate seeds scattered over the top.

Whole Wheat Pizza

Servings: 2
Cooking Time:xx
Ingredients:

- 100g marinara sauce
- 2 whole wheat pitta
- 200g baby spinach leaves
- 1 small plum tomato, sliced
- 1 clove garlic, sliced
- 400g grated cheese
- 50g shaved parmesan

Directions:

1. Preheat air fryer to 160°C
2. Spread each of the pitta with marinara sauce
3. Sprinkle with cheese, top with spinach, plum tomato and garlic. Finish with parmesan shavings
4. Place in the air fryer and cook for about 4 mins cheese has melted

Quinoa-stuffed Romano Peppers

Servings: 2
Cooking Time:xx
Ingredients:

- 1 tablespoon olive oil
- 1 onion, diced
- 1 garlic clove, chopped
- 100 g/⅔ cup uncooked quinoa
- 1½ tablespoons fajita seasoning
- 140 g/1 cup canned sweetcorn/corn kernels (drained weight)
- 3 romano peppers, sliced lengthways, seeds removed but stalk left intact
- 60 g/⅔ cup grated mature Cheddar

Directions:

1. Heat the oil in a saucepan. Add the onion and garlic and sauté for 5 minutes, until soft. Add the quinoa, fajita seasoning and 250 ml/1 cup water. Bring to a simmer, then cover with a lid and simmer for 15 minutes or until the quinoa is cooked and the water absorbed. Stir in the sweetcorn/corn kernels. Stuff each pepper half with the quinoa mixture, then top with grated cheese.
2. Preheat the air-fryer to 180°C/350°F.
3. Place the peppers on an air-fryer liner or a piece of pierced parchment paper, place in the preheated air-fryer and air-fry for 12–14 minutes, depending how 'chargrilled' you like your peppers.

Goat's Cheese Tartlets

Servings: 2
Cooking Time:xx
Ingredients:

- 1 readymade sheet of puff pastry, 35 x 23 cm/14 x 9 in. (gluten-free if you wish)
- 4 tablespoons pesto (jarred or see page 80)
- 4 roasted baby (bell) peppers (see page 120)
- 4 tablespoons soft goat's cheese
- 2 teaspoons milk (plant-based if you wish)

Directions:

1. Cut the pastry sheet in half along the long edge, to make two smaller rectangles. Fold in the edges of each pastry rectangle to form a crust. Using a fork, prick a few holes in the base of the pastry. Brush half the pesto onto each rectangle, top with the peppers and goat's cheese. Brush the pastry crust with milk.
2. Preheat the air-fryer to 180°C/350°F.
3. Place one tartlet on an air-fryer liner or a piece of pierced parchment paper in the preheated air-fryer and air-fry for 6 minutes (you'll need to cook them one at a time). Repeat with the second tartlet.

Air Fryer Cheese Sandwich

Servings:2
Cooking Time:10 Minutes
Ingredients:

- 4 slices white or wholemeal bread
- 2 tbsp butter
- 50 g / 3.5 oz cheddar cheese, grated

Directions:

1. Preheat the air fryer to 180 °C / 350 °F and line the bottom of the basket with parchment paper.
2. Lay the slices of bread out on a clean surface and butter one side of each. Evenly sprinkle the cheese on two of the slices and cover with the final two slices.
3. Transfer the sandwiches to the air fryer, close the lid, and cook for 5 minutes until the bread is crispy and golden, and the cheese is melted.

Mini Quiche

Servings: 2
Cooking Time:xx

Ingredients:

- 100g raw cashews
- 3 tbsp milk
- ½ tsp hot sauce
- 1 tsp white miso paste
- 1 tsp mustard
- 300g tofu
- 100g bacon pieces
- 1 chopped red pepper
- 1 chopped onion
- 6 tbsp yeast
- ½ tsp onion powder
- ½ tsp paprika
- ½ tsp cumin
- ½ tsp chilli powder
- ½ tsp black pepper
- ⅛ tsp turmeric
- ½ tsp canola oil
- 50g curly kale

Directions:

1. Heat the oil in a pan, add the bacon pepper, onion and curly kale and cook for about 3 minutes
2. Place all the other ingredients into a blender and blend until smooth
3. Add to a bowl with the bacon, pepper, onion and curly kale and mix well
4. Fill silicone muffin cups with the mix
5. Place in the air fryer and cook at 165°C for 15 minutes

Spinach And Feta Croissants

Servings:4
Cooking Time:10 Minutes

Ingredients:

- 4 pre-made croissants
- 100 g / 7 oz feta cheese, crumbled
- 1 tsp dried chives
- 1 tsp garlic powder
- 50 g / 3.5 oz fresh spinach, chopped

Directions:

1. Preheat the air fryer to 180 °C / 350 °F. Remove the mesh basket from the air fryer machine and line with parchment paper.
2. Cut the croissants in half and lay each half out on the lined mesh basket.
3. In a bowl, combine the crumbled feta cheese, dried chives, garlic powder, and chopped spinach until they form a consistent mixture.
4. Spoon some of the mixture one half of the four croissants and cover with the second half of the croissants to seal in the filling.
5. Carefully slide the croissants in the mesh basket into the air fryer machine, close the lid, and cook for 10 minutes until the pastry is crispy and the feta cheese has melted.

Butternut Squash Falafel

Servings: 2
Cooking Time:xx
Ingredients:

- 500 g/1 lb. 2 oz. frozen butternut squash cubes
- 1 tablespoon olive oil, plus extra for cooking
- 100 g/¾ cup canned or cooked chickpeas (drained weight)
- 20 g/¼ cup gram/chickpea flour
- 1 teaspoon ground cumin
- ½ teaspoon ground coriander
- ½ teaspoon salt

Directions:

1. Preheat the air-fryer to 180°C/350°F.
2. Toss the frozen butternut squash in the olive oil. Add to the preheated air-fryer and air-fry for 12–14 minutes, until soft but not caramelized. Remove from the air-fryer and mash the squash by hand or using a food processor, then combine with the chickpeas, flour, spices and salt. Leave the mixture to cool, then divide into 6 equal portions and mould into patties.
3. Preheat the air-fryer to 180°C/350°F.
4. Spray the patties with a little olive oil, then add to the preheated air-fryer and air-fry for 10 minutes, turning once (carefully) during cooking. Enjoy hot or cold.

Sticky Tofu With Cauliflower Rice

Servings:4
Cooking Time:20 Minutes
Ingredients:

- For the tofu:
- 1 x 180 g / 6 oz block firm tofu
- 2 tbsp soy sauce
- 1 onion, sliced
- 1 large carrot, peeled and thinly sliced
- For the cauliflower:
- 200 g / 7 oz cauliflower florets
- 2 tbsp soy sauce
- 1 tbsp sesame oil
- 2 cloves garlic, minced
- 100 g / 3.5 oz broccoli, chopped into small florets

Directions:

1. Preheat the air fryer to 190 °C / 370 °F and line the air fryer with parchment paper or grease it with olive oil.
2. Crumble the tofu into a bowl and mix in the soy sauce, and the sliced onion and carrot.
3. Cook the tofu and vegetables in the air fryer for 10 minutes.
4. Meanwhile, place the cauliflower florets into a blender and pulse until it forms a rice-like consistency.
5. Place the cauliflower rice in a bowl and mix in the soy sauce, sesame oil, minced garlic cloves, and broccoli florets until well combined. Transfer to the air fryer and cook for 10 minutes until hot and crispy.

Sweet Potato Taquitos

Servings: 10
Cooking Time:xx
Ingredients:

- 1 sweet potato cut into ½ inch pieces
- 1 ½ tsp oil
- 1 chopped onion
- 1 tsp minced garlic
- 400g black beans
- 3 tbsp water
- 10 corn tortillas
- 1 chipotle pepper, chopped
- ½ tsp cumin
- ½ tsp paprika
- ½ chilli powder
- ⅛ tsp salt
- ½ tsp maple syrup

Directions:

1. Place the sweet potato in the air fryer spray with oil and cook for 12 minutes at 200°C
2. Heat oil in a pan, add the onion and garlic and cook for a few minutes until soft
3. Add remaining ingredients to the pan, add 2 tbsp of water and combine
4. Add the sweet potato and 1 tbsp of water and mix
5. Warm the tortilla in the microwave for about 1 minute
6. Place a row of filling across the centre of each tortilla. Fold up the bottom of the tortilla, tuck under the filling, fold in the edges then continue to roll the tortilla
7. Place in the air fryer and cook for about 12 minutes

Ravioli Air Fryer Style

Servings: 4
Cooking Time:xx
Ingredients:

- Half a pack of frozen ravioli
- 200g Italian breadcrumbs
- 200ml buttermilk
- 5 tbsp marinara sauce
- 1 tbsp olive oil

Directions:

1. Preheat the air fryer to 220°C
2. Place the buttermilk in a bowl
3. Add the breadcrumbs to another bowl
4. Take each piece of ravioli and dip it first into the buttermilk and then into the breadcrumbs, coating evenly
5. Add the ravioli to the air fryer and cook for 7 minutes, adding a small amount of oil at the halfway point
6. Serve with the marinara sauce on the side

Shakshuka

Servings: 2
Cooking Time:xx

Ingredients:

- 2 eggs
- BASE
- 100 g/3½ oz. thinly sliced (bell) peppers
- 1 red onion, halved and thinly sliced
- 2 medium tomatoes, chopped
- 2 teaspoons olive oil
- ¼ teaspoon salt
- ¼ teaspoon freshly ground black pepper
- ½ teaspoon chilli/hot red pepper flakes
- SAUCE
- 100 g/3½ oz. passata/strained tomatoes
- 1 tablespoon tomato purée/paste
- 1 teaspoon balsamic vinegar
- ½ teaspoon runny honey
- ½ teaspoon ground cumin
- ½ teaspoon paprika
- ¼ teaspoon salt
- ⅛ teaspoon freshly ground black pepper

Directions:

1. Preheat the air-fryer to 180°C/350°F.
2. Combine the base ingredients together in a baking dish that fits inside your air-fryer. Add the dish to the preheated air-fryer and air-fry for 10 minutes, stirring halfway through cooking.
3. Meanwhile, combine the sauce ingredients in a bowl. Pour this into the baking dish when the 10 minutes are up. Stir, then make a couple of wells in the sauce for the eggs. Crack the eggs into the wells, then cook for a further 5 minutes or until the eggs are just cooked and yolks still runny. Remove from the air-fryer and serve.

Bbq Soy Curls

Servings: 2
Cooking Time:xx

Ingredients:

- 250ml warm water
- 1 tsp vegetable bouillon
- 200g soy curls
- 40g BBQ sauce
- 1 tsp oil

Directions:

1. Soak the soy curls in water and bouillon for 10 minutes
2. Place the soy curls in another bowl and shred
3. Heat the air fryer to 200°C
4. Cook for 3 minutes
5. Remove from the air fryer and coat in bbq sauce
6. Return to the air fryer and cook for 5 minutes shaking halfway through

Gnocchi Caprese

Servings: 2
Cooking Time:xx

Ingredients:

- 1 packet of gnocchi
- 150g cherry tomatoes, cut into halves
- 2 tbsp olive oil
- 2 tbsp balsamic vinegar
- 3 pressed cloves of garlic
- 200g basil, chopped
- 200g mini mozzarella balls
- 150g grated Parmesan
- Salt and pepper for seasoning

Directions:

1. Preheat the air fryer to 220°C
2. Take a large bowl and add the cherry tomatoes, gnocchi, oil, balsamic vinegar, garlic and seasoning, making sure that everything is well coated
3. Transfer to the air fryer basket
4. Cook for 10 minutes, shaking the basket every few minutes
5. Once cooked, transfer everything to a large mixing bowl and add the Parmesan cheese, coating well
6. Then, add the mozzarella and basil and toss once more

Miso Mushrooms On Sourdough Toast

Servings: 1
Cooking Time:xx

Ingredients:

- 1 teaspoon miso paste
- 1 teaspoon oil, such as avocado or coconut (melted)
- 1 teaspoon soy sauce
- 80 g/3 oz. chestnut mushrooms, sliced 5 mm/½ in. thick
- 1 large slice sourdough bread
- 2 teaspoons butter or plant-based spread
- a little freshly chopped flat-leaf parsley, to serve

Directions:

1. Preheat the air-fryer to 200°C/400°F.
2. In a small bowl or ramekin mix together the miso paste, oil and soy sauce.
3. Place the mushrooms in a small shallow gratin dish that fits inside your air-fryer. Add the sauce to the mushrooms and mix together. Place the gratin dish in the preheated air-fryer and air-fry for 6–7 minutes, stirring once during cooking.
4. With 4 minutes left to cook, add the bread to the air-fryer and turn over at 2 minutes whilst giving the mushrooms a final stir.
5. Once cooked, butter the toast and serve the mushrooms on top, scattered with chopped parsley.

Tofu Bowls

Servings: 4
Cooking Time:xx

Ingredients:

- 1 block of tofu, cut into cubes
- 40ml soy sauce
- 2 tbsp sesame oil
- 1 tsp garlic powder
- 1 chopped onion
- 2 tbsp Tahini dressing
- 3 bunches baby bok choy, chopped
- 300g quinoa
- 1 medium cucumber, sliced
- 1 cup shredded carrot
- 1 avocado, sliced

Directions:

1. Mix the soy sauce, 1 tbsp sesame oil and garlic powder in a bowl. Add the tofu marinade for 10 minutes
2. Place in the air fryer and cook at 200°C for 20 minutes turning halfway
3. Heat the remaining sesame oil in a pan and cook the onions for about 4 minutes
4. Add the bok choy and cook for another 4 minutes
5. Divide the quinoa between your bowls add bok choy, carrot, cucumber and avocado. Top with the tofu and drizzle with Tahini

Cheese, Tomato & Pesto Crustless Quiches

Servings: 1–2
Cooking Time:xx

Ingredients:

- 40 g/½ cup grated mature Cheddar
- 3 eggs, beaten
- 3 cherry tomatoes, finely chopped
- salt and freshly ground black pepper
- ½ teaspoon olive oil, to grease ramekins
- 2 tablespoons pesto (jarred or see page 80)

Directions:

1. Preheat the air-fryer to 180°C/350°F.
2. Mix together the cheese, eggs, tomatoes, salt and pepper in a bowl.
3. Grease the ramekins with the oil (and line with parchment paper if you wish to remove the quiches to serve). Pour the egg mixture into the ramekins.
4. Place the ramekins in the preheated air-fryer and air-fry for 10 minutes, stirring the contents of the ramekins halfway through cooking. Serve hot with 1 tablespoon pesto drizzled over each quiche.

Courgette Meatballs

Servings: 4
Cooking Time:xx
Ingredients:

- 400g oats
- 40g feta, crumbled
- 1 beaten egg
- Salt and pepper
- 150g courgette
- 1 tsp lemon rind
- 6 basil leaves, thinly sliced
- 1 tsp dill
- 1 tsp oregano

Directions:

1. Preheat the air fryer to 200°C
2. Grate the courgette into a bowl, squeeze any access water out
3. Add all the remaining ingredients apart from the oats and mix well
4. Blend the oats until they resemble breadcrumbs
5. Add the oats into the other mix and stir well
6. Form into balls and place in the air fryer cook for 10 minutes

Tempura Veggies

Servings: 4
Cooking Time:xx
Ingredients:

- 150g flour
- ½ tsp salt
- ½ tsp pepper
- 2 eggs
- 2 tbsp cup water
- 100g avocado wedges
- 100g courgette slices
- 100g panko breadcrumbs
- 2 tsp oil
- 100g green beans
- 100g asparagus spears
- 100g red onion rings
- 100g pepper rings

Directions:

1. Mix together flour, salt and pepper. In another bowl mix eggs and water
2. Stir together panko crumbs and oil in a separate bowl
3. Dip vegetables in the flour mix, then egg and then the bread crumbs
4. Preheat the air fryer to 200°C
5. Place in the air fryer and cook for about 10 minutes until golden brown

Sauces & Snack And Appetiser Recipes

Bacon Smokies

Servings: 8
Cooking Time:xx
Ingredients:

- 150g little smokies (pieces)
- 150g bacon
- 50g brown sugar
- Toothpicks

Directions:

1. Cut the bacon strips into thirds
2. Put the brown sugar into a bowl
3. Coat the bacon with the sugar
4. Wrap the bacon around the little smokies and secure with a toothpick
5. Heat the air fryer to 170°C
6. Place in the air fryer and cook for 10 minutes until crispy

Garlic Cheese Bread

Servings: 2
Cooking Time:xx
Ingredients:

- 250g grated mozzarella
- 50g grated parmesan
- 1 egg
- ½ tsp garlic powder

Directions:

1. Line air fryer with parchment paper
2. Mix ingredients in a bowl
3. Press into a circle onto the parchment paper in the air fryer
4. Heat the air fryer to 175°C
5. Cook for 10 minutes

Korean Chicken Wings

Servings: 2
Cooking Time:xx
Ingredients:

- 25ml soy sauce
- 40g brown sugar
- 2 tbsp hot pepper paste
- 1 tsp sesame oil
- ½ tsp ginger paste
- ½ tsp garlic paste
- 2 green onions, chopped
- 400g chicken wings
- 1 tbsp vegetable oil

Directions:

1. Preheat air fryer to 200°C
2. Place all ingredients apart from chicken wings and vegetable oil in a pan and simmer for about 4 minutes set aside
3. Massage the vegetable oil into the chicken wings
4. Place in the air fryer and cook for about 10 minutes
5. Turn and cook for a further 10 minutes
6. Coat the wings in the sauce and return to the air fryer
7. Cook for about 2 minutes

Waffle Fries

Servings: 4
Cooking Time:xx
Ingredients:

- 2 large potatoes, russet potatoes work best
- 1 tsp salt for seasoning
- Waffle cutter

Directions:

1. Peel the potatoes and slice using the waffle cutter. You can also use a mandolin cutter that has a blade
2. Transfer the potatoes to a bowl and season with the salt, coating evenly
3. Add to the air fryer and cook at 220°C for 15 minutes, shaking every so often

Pretzel Bites

Servings: 2
Cooking Time:xx

Ingredients:

- 650g flour
- 2.5 tsp active dry yeast
- 260ml hot water
- 1 tsp salt
- 4 tbsp melted butter
- 2 tbsp sugar

Directions:

1. Take a large bowl and add the flour, sugar and salt
2. Take another bowl and combine the hot water and yeast, stirring until the yeast has dissolved
3. Then, add the yeast mixture to the flour mixture and use your hands to combine
4. Knead for 2 minutes
5. Cover the bowl with a kitchen towel for around half an hour
6. Divide the dough into 6 pieces
7. Preheat the air fryer to 260°C
8. Take each section of dough and tear off a piece, rolling it in your hands to create a rope shape, that is around 1" in thickness
9. Cut into 2" strips
10. Place the small dough balls into the air fryer and leave a little space in-between
11. Cook for 6 minutes
12. Once cooked, remove and brush with melted butter and sprinkle salt on top

Onion Pakoda

Servings: 2
Cooking Time:xx

Ingredients:

- 200g gram flour
- 2 onions, thinly sliced
- 1 tbsp crushed coriander seeds
- 1 tsp chilli powder
- ¾ tsp salt
- ¼ tsp turmeric
- ¼ tsp baking soda

Directions:

1. Mix all the ingredients together in a large bowl
2. Make bite sized pakodas
3. Heat the air fryer to 200°C
4. Line the air fryer with foil
5. Place the pakoda in the air fryer and cook for 5 minutes
6. Turn over and cook for a further 5 minutes

Chicken & Bacon Parcels

Servings: 4
Cooking Time:xx
Ingredients:

- 2 chicken breasts, boneless and skinless
- 200ml BBQ sauce
- 7 slices of bacon, cut lengthwise into halves
- 2 tbsp brown sugar

Directions:

1. Preheat the air fryer to 220°C
2. Cut the chicken into strips, you should have 7 in total
3. Wrap two strips of the bacon around each piece of chicken
4. Brush the BBQ sauce over the top and sprinkle with the brown sugar
5. Place the chicken into the basket and cook for 5 minutes
6. Turn the chicken over and cook for another 5 minutes

Garlic Pizza Toast

Servings: 8
Cooking Time:xx
Ingredients:

- 1 pack garlic Texas toast, or 8 slices of bread topped with garlic butter
- 100g pizza sauce
- 50g pepperoni
- 100g grated cheese

Directions:

1. Top each piece of toast with pizza sauce
2. Add cheese and pepperoni
3. Heat air fryer to 190°C
4. Place in the air fryer and cook for 5 minutes

Jalapeño Poppers

Servings: 2
Cooking Time:xx
Ingredients:

- 10 jalapeños, halved and deseeded
- 100g cream cheese
- 50g parsley
- 150g breadcrumbs

Directions:

1. Mix 1/2 the breadcrumbs with the cream cheese
2. Add the parsley
3. Stuff the peppers with the cream cheese mix
4. Top the peppers with the remaining breadcrumbs
5. Heat the air fryer to 185°C
6. Place in the air fryer and cook for 6-8 minutes

Mozzarella Sticks

Servings: 4
Cooking Time:xx
Ingredients:

- 60ml water
- 50g flour
- 5 tbsp cornstarch
- 1 tbsp cornmeal
- 1 tsp garlic powder
- ½ tsp salt
- 100g breadcrumbs
- ½ tsp pepper
- ½ tsp parsley
- ½ tsp onion powder
- ¼ tsp oregano
- ½ tsp basil
- 200g mozzarella cut into ½ inch strips

Directions:

1. Mix water, flour, cornstarch, cornmeal, garlic powder and salt in a bowl
2. Stir breadcrumbs, pepper, parsley, onion powder, oregano and basil together in another bowl
3. Dip the mozzarella sticks in the batter then coat in the breadcrumbs
4. Heat the air fryer to 200°C
5. Cook for 6 minutes turn and cook for another 6 minutes

Tasty Pumpkin Seeds

Servings: 2
Cooking Time:xx
Ingredients:

- 1 ¾ cups pumpkin seeds
- 2 tsp avocado oil
- 1 tsp paprika
- 1 tsp salt

Directions:

1. Preheat air fryer to 180°C
2. Add all ingredients to a bowl and mix well
3. Place in the air fryer and cook for 35 minutes shaking frequently

Salt And Vinegar Chips

Servings: 4
Cooking Time:xx
Ingredients:

- 6-10 Jerusalem artichokes, thinly sliced
- 150ml apple cider vinegar
- 2 tbsp olive oil
- Sea salt

Directions:

1. Soak the artichoke in apple cider vinegar for 20-30 minutes
2. Preheat the air fryer to 200°C
3. Coat the artichoke in olive oil
4. Place in the air fryer and cook for 15 Minutes
5. Sprinkle with salt

Mac & Cheese Bites

Servings: 14
Cooking Time:xx
Ingredients:

- 200g mac and cheese
- 2 eggs
- 200g panko breadcrumbs
- Cooking spray

Directions:

1. Place drops of mac and cheese on parchment paper and freeze for 1 hour
2. Beat the eggs in a bowl, add the breadcrumbs to another bowl
3. Dip the mac and cheese balls in the egg then into the breadcrumbs
4. Heat the air fryer to 190°C
5. Place in the air fryer, spray with cooking spray and cook for 15 minutes

Pepperoni Bread

Servings: 4
Cooking Time:xx
Ingredients:

- Cooking spray
- 400g pizza dough
- 200g pepperoni
- 1 tbsp dried oregano
- Ground pepper to taste
- Garlic salt to taste
- 1 tsp melted butter
- 1 tsp grated parmesan
- 50g grated mozzarella

Directions:

1. Line a baking tin with 2 inch sides with foil to fit in the air fryer
2. Spray with cooking spray
3. Preheat the air fryer to 200°C
4. Roll the pizza dough into 1 inch balls and line the baking tin
5. Sprinkle with pepperoni, oregano, pepper and garlic salt
6. Brush with melted butter and sprinkle with parmesan
7. Place in the air fryer and cook for 15 minutes
8. Sprinkle with mozzarella and cook for another 2 minutes

Onion Bahji

Servings: 8
Cooking Time:xx
Ingredients:

- 1 sliced red onion
- 1 sliced onion
- 1 tsp salt
- 1 minced jalapeño pepper
- 150g chickpea flour
- 4 tbsp water
- 1 clove garlic, minced
- 1 tsp coriander
- 1 tsp chilli powder
- 1 tsp turmeric
- ½ tsp cumin

Directions:

1. Place all ingredients in a bowl and mix well, leave to rest for 10 minutes
2. Preheat air fryer to 175°C
3. Spray air fryer with cooking spray.
4. Form mix into bahji shapes and add to air fryer
5. Cook for 6 minutes turn and cook for a further 6 minutes

Tortellini Bites

Servings: 6
Cooking Time:xx
Ingredients:

- 200g cheese tortellini
- 150g flour
- 100g panko bread crumbs
- 50g grated parmesan
- 1 tsp dried oregano
- 2 eggs
- ½ tsp garlic powder
- ½ tsp chilli flakes
- Salt
- Pepper

Directions:

1. Cook the tortellini according to the packet instructions
2. Mix the panko, parmesan, oregano, garlic powder, chilli flakes salt and pepper in a bowl
3. Beat the eggs in another bowl and place the flour in a third bowl
4. Coat the tortellini in flour, then egg and then in the panko mix
5. Place in the air fryer and cook at 185°C for 10 minutes until crispy
6. Serve with marinara sauce for dipping

Popcorn Tofu

Servings: 4
Cooking Time:xx

Ingredients:

- 400g firm tofu
- 100g chickpea flour
- 100g oatmeal
- 2 tbsp yeast
- 150ml milk
- 400g breadcrumbs
- 1 tsp garlic powder
- 1 tsp onion powder
- 1 tbsp dijon mustard
- ½ tsp salt
- ½ tsp pepper
- 2 tbsp vegetable bouillon

Directions:

1. Rip the tofu into pieces. Place the breadcrumbs into a bowl, in another bowl mix the remaining ingredients
2. Dip the tofu into the batter mix and then dip into the breadcrumbs
3. Heat the air fryer to 175°C
4. Place the tofu in the air fryer and cook for 12 minutes shaking halfway through

Corn Nuts

Servings: 8
Cooking Time:xx

Ingredients:

- 1 giant white corn
- 3 tbsp vegetable oil
- 2 tsp salt

Directions:

1. Place the corn in a large bowl, cover with water and sit for 8 hours
2. Drain, pat dry and air dry for 20 minutes
3. Preheat the air fryer to 200°C
4. Place in a bowl and coat with oil and salt
5. Cook in the air fryer for 10 minutes shake then cook for a further 10 minutes

Italian Rice Balls

Servings: 2
Cooking Time:xx
Ingredients:

- 400g cooked rice
- 25g breadcrumbs, plus an extra 200g for breading
- 2 tbsp flour, plus an extra 2 tbsp for breading
- 1 tbsp cornstarch, plus an extra 3 tbsp for breading
- 1 chopped bell pepper
- 1 chopped onion
- 2 tbsp olive oil
- 1 tsp red chilli flakes
- 5 chopped mozzarella cheese sticks
- A little water for the breading
- Salt and pepper for seasoning

Directions:

1. Place the cooked rice into a bowl and mash with a fork. Place to one side
2. Take a saucepan and add the oil, salting the onion and peppers until they're both soft
3. Add the chilli flakes and a little salt and combine
4. Add the mixture to the mashed rice and combine
5. Add the 2 tbsp flour and 1 tbsp cornstarch, along with the 25g breadcrumbs and combine well
6. Use your hands to create balls with the mixture
7. Stuff a piece of the mozzarella inside the balls and form around it
8. Take a bowl and add the rest of the flour, corn starch and a little seasoning, with a small amount of water to create a thick batter
9. Take another bowl and add the rest of the breadcrumbs
10. Dip each rice ball into the batter and then the breadcrumbs
11. Preheat the air fryer to 220°C
12. Cook for 6 minutes, before shaking and cooking for another 6 minutes

Spicy Peanuts

Servings: 8
Cooking Time:xx
Ingredients:

- 2 tbsp olive oil
- 3 tbsp seafood seasoning
- ½ tsp cayenne
- 300g raw peanuts
- Salt to taste

Directions:

1. Preheat the air fryer to 160°C
2. Whisk together ingredients in a bowl and stir in the peanuts
3. Add to air fryer and cook for 10 minutes, shake then cook for a further 10 minutes
4. Sprinkle with salt and cook for another 5 minutes

Cheese Wontons

Servings: 8
Cooking Time:xx

Ingredients:

- 8 wonton wrappers
- 1 carton pimento cheese
- Small dish of water
- Cooking spray

Directions:

1. Place one tsp of cheese in the middle of each wonton wrapper
2. Brush the edges of each wonton wrapper with water
3. Fold over to create a triangle and seal
4. Heat the air fryer to 190°C
5. Spray the wontons with cooking spray
6. Place in the air fryer and cook for 3 minutes
7. Turnover and cook for a further 3 minutes

Scotch Eggs

Servings: 6
Cooking Time:xx

Ingredients:

- 300g pork sausage
- 6 hard boiled eggs, shelled
- 50g cup flour
- 2 eggs, beaten
- 1 cup breadcrumbs
- Cooking spray

Directions:

1. Divide sausage into 6 portions
2. Place an egg in the middle of each portion and wrap around the egg
3. Dip the sausage in flour, then egg and then coat in breadcrumbs
4. Place in the air fryer and cook at 200°C for 12 minutes

Fish & Seafood Recipes

Pesto Salmon

Servings: 4
Cooking Time:xx
Ingredients:

- 4 x 150–175-g/5½–6-oz. salmon fillets
- lemon wedges, to serve
- PESTO
- 50 g/scant ½ cup toasted pine nuts
- 50 g/2 oz. fresh basil
- 50 g/⅔ cup grated Parmesan or Pecorino
- 100 ml/7 tablespoons olive oil

Directions:

1. To make the pesto, blitz the pine nuts, basil and Parmesan to a paste in a food processor. Pour in the olive oil and process again.
2. Preheat the air-fryer to 160°C/325°F.
3. Top each salmon fillet with 2 tablespoons of the pesto. Add the salmon fillets to the preheated air-fryer and air-fry for 9 minutes. Check the internal temperature of the fish has reached at least 63°C/145°F using a meat thermometer – if not, cook for another few minutes.

Coconut Shrimp

Servings: 4
Cooking Time:xx
Ingredients:

- 250g flour
- 1 ½ tsp black pepper
- 2 eggs
- 150g unsweetened flaked coconut
- 1 Serrano chilli, thinly sliced
- 25g panko bread crumbs
- 300g shrimp raw
- ½ tsp salt
- 4 tbsp honey
- 25ml lime juice

Directions:

1. Mix together flour and pepper, in another bowl beat the eggs and in another bowl mix the panko and coconut
2. Dip each of the shrimp in the flour mix then the egg and then cover in the coconut mix
3. Coat the shrimp in cooking spray
4. Place in the air fryer and cook at 200°C for 6-8 mins turning half way through
5. Mix together the honey, lime juice and chilli and serve with the shrimp

Tilapia Fillets

Servings: 2
Cooking Time:xx
Ingredients:

- 2 tbsp melted butter
- 150g almond flour
- 3 tbsp mayonnaise
- 2tilapia fillets
- 25g thinly sliced almonds
- Salt and pepper to taste
- Vegetable oil spray

Directions:

1. Mix the almond flour, butter, pepper and salt together in a bowl
2. Spread mayonnaise on both sides of the fish
3. Cover the fillets in the almond flour mix
4. Spread one side of the fish with the sliced almonds
5. Spray the air fryer with the vegetable spray
6. Place in the air fryer and cook at 160°C for 10 minutes

Fish Taco Cauliflower Rice Bowls

Servings: 2
Cooking Time:xx
Ingredients:

- 400g fish of your choice, cut into strips
- 1 tsp chilli powder
- ½ tsp paprika
- 1 sliced avocado
- 25g pickled red onions
- 25g reduced fat sour cream
- ½ tsp cumin
- Salt and pepper to taste
- 300g cauliflower rice
- 1 tbsp lime juice
- 25g fresh coriander
- 1 tbsp sriracha

Directions:

1. Sprinkle both sides of the fish with chilli powder, cumin, paprika, salt and pepper
2. Heat the air fryer to 200°C, cook the fish for about 12 minutes
3. cook the cauliflower rice according to instructions, mix in lime juice and coriander once cooked
4. Divide the cauliflower rice between two bowls, add the sliced avocado, fish and pickled red onions.
5. Mix the sour cream with the sriracha and drizzle over the top

Shrimp Wrapped With Bacon

Servings: 2
Cooking Time:xx
Ingredients:

- 16 shrimp
- 16 slices of bacon
- 2 tbsp ranch dressing to serve

Directions:

1. Preheat the air fryer to 200°C
2. Wrap the shrimps in the bacon
3. Refrigerate for 30 minutes
4. Cook the shrimp for about 5 minutes turn them over and cook for a further 2 minutes
5. Serve with the ranch dressing on the side

Shrimp With Yum Yum Sauce

Servings: 4
Cooking Time:xx
Ingredients:

- 400g peeled jumbo shrimp
- 1 tbsp soy sauce
- 1 tbsp garlic paste
- 1 tbsp ginger paste
- 4 tbsp mayo
- 2 tbsp ketchup
- 1 tbsp sugar
- 1 tsp paprika
- 1 tsp garlic powder

Directions:

1. Mix soy sauce, garlic paste and ginger paste in a bowl. Add the shrimp, allow to marinate for 15 minutes
2. In another bowl mix ketchup, mayo, sugar, paprika and the garlic powder to make the yum yum sauce.
3. Set the air fryer to 200°C, place shrimp in the basket and cook for 8-10 minutes

Fish Sticks With Tartar Sauce Batter

Servings: 4
Cooking Time:xx
Ingredients:

- 6 tbsp mayonnaise
- 2 tbsp dill pickle
- 1 tsp seafood seasoning
- 400g cod fillets, cut into sticks
- 300g panko breadcrumbs

Directions:

1. Combine the mayonnaise, seafood seasoning and dill pickle in a large bowl.
2. Add the cod sticks and coat well
3. Preheat air fryer to 200°C
4. Coat the fish sticks in the breadcrumbs
5. Place in the air fryer and cook for 12 minutes

Crunchy Fish

Servings: 4
Cooking Time:xx
Ingredients:

- 200g dry breadcrumbs
- 4 tbsp olive oil
- 4 fillets of white fish
- 1 beaten egg
- 1 sliced lemon

Directions:

1. Heat the fryer to 180°C
2. In a medium mixing bowl, combine the olive oil and the breadcrumbs
3. Take the fish and first dip it into the egg and then the breadcrumbs, making sure they are evenly coated well
4. Arrange the fish into the basket
5. Cook for 12 minutes
6. Remove and serve with lemon slices

Crispy Nacho Prawns

Servings: 6
Cooking Time:xx
Ingredients:

- 1 egg
- 18 large prawns
- 1 bag of nacho cheese flavoured corn chips, crushed

Directions:

1. Wash the prawns and pat dry
2. Place the chips into a bowl
3. In another bowl, whisk the egg
4. Dip the prawns into the egg and then the nachos
5. Preheat the air fryer to 180°C
6. Cook for 8 minutes

Fish In Parchment Paper

Servings: 2
Cooking Time:xx
Ingredients:

- 250g cod fillets
- 1 chopped carrot
- 1 chopped fennel
- 1 tbsp oil
- 1 thinly sliced red pepper
- ½ tsp tarragon
- 1 tbsp lemon juice
- 1 tbsp salt
- ½ tsp ground pepper

Directions:

1. In a bowl, mix the tarragon and ½ tsp salt add the vegetables and mix well
2. Cut two large squares of parchment paper
3. Spray the cod with oil and cover both sides with salt and pepper
4. Place the cod in the parchment paper and add the vegetables
5. Fold over the paper to hold the fish and vegetables
6. Place in the air fryer and cook at 170°C for 15 minutes

Baked Panko Cod

Servings: 5
Cooking Time:xx

Ingredients:

- 400g cod, cut into 5 pieces
- 250g panko breadcrumbs
- 1 egg plus 1 egg white extra
- Cooking spray
- ½ tsp onion powder
- ½ tsp garlic salt
- ⅛ tsp black pepper
- ½ tsp mixed herbs

Directions:

1. Heat air fryer to 220°C
2. Beat the egg and egg white in a bowl
3. Sprinkle fish with herbs and spice mix, dip into the egg and then cover in the panko bread crumbs
4. Line air fryer basket with tin foil. Place the fish in the air fryer and coat with cooking spray
5. Cook for about 15 minutes until, fish is lightly browned

Parmesan-coated Fish Fingers

Servings: 2
Cooking Time:xx

Ingredients:

- 350 g/12 oz. cod loins
- 1 tablespoon grated Parmesan
- 40 g/½ cup dried breadcrumbs (gluten-free if you wish, see page 9)
- 1 egg, beaten
- 2 tablespoons plain/all-purpose flour (gluten free if you wish)

Directions:

1. Slice the cod into 6 equal fish fingers/sticks.
2. Mix the Parmesan together with the breadcrumbs. Lay out three bowls: one with flour, one with beaten egg and the other with the Parmesan breadcrumbs. Dip each fish finger/stick first into the flour, then the egg and then the breadcrumbs until fully coated.
3. Preheat the air-fryer to 180°C/350°F.
4. Add the fish to the preheated air-fryer and air-fry for 6 minutes. Check the internal temperature of the fish has reached at least 75°C/167°F using a meat thermometer – if not, cook for another few minutes. Serve immediately.

Gluten Free Honey And Garlic Shrimp

Servings: 2
Cooking Time:xx
Ingredients:

- 500g fresh shrimp
- 5 tbsp honey
- 2 tbsp gluten free soy sauce
- 2 tbsp tomato ketchup
- 250g frozen stir fry vegetables
- 1 crushed garlic clove
- 1 tsp fresh ginger
- 2 tbsp cornstarch

Directions:

1. Simmer the honey, soy sauce, garlic, tomato ketchup and ginger in a saucepan
2. Add the cornstarch and whisk until sauce thickens
3. Coat the shrimp with the sauce
4. Line the air fryer with foil and add the shrimp and vegetables
5. Cook at 180°C for 10 minutes

Tandoori Salmon

Servings: 4
Cooking Time:xx
Ingredients:

- 300g salmon
- 1 tbsp butter
- 1 tbsp tandoori spice
- Salt and pepper to taste
- 1 small tomato
- Half a red onion
- 600g plain yogurt
- 30 fresh mint leaves, chopped
- 1 tsp minced green chilli
- 1 tbsp ground cumin
- Half a cucumber, chopped

Directions:

1. Cut the salmon into cubes and coat in the tandoori spice mix. Chill for 30 minutes to marinate
2. Blend mint, cumin and chilli with ¼ of the yogurt refrigerate and leave to steep
3. Peel the tomato and cut into cubes. Peel the cucumber and chop into cubes, finely dice the onion
4. Cook the salmon in the air fryer for 5-6 minutes at 200°C
5. Mix the flavoured yogurt with the remaining yogurt, tomato, cucumber and onion
6. Place the sauce in serving bowls and place the salmon on top

Garlic-parsley Prawns

Servings: 2
Cooking Time:xx

Ingredients:

- 300 g/10½ oz. raw king prawns/jumbo shrimp (without shell)
- 40 g/3 tablespoons garlic butter, softened (see page 72)
- 2 tablespoons freshly chopped flat-leaf parsley

Directions:

1. Thread the prawns/shrimp onto 6 metal skewers that will fit your air-fryer. Mix together the softened garlic butter and parsley and brush evenly onto the prawn skewers.
2. Preheat the air-fryer to 180°C/350°F.
3. Place the skewers on an air-fryer liner or a piece of pierced parchment paper. Add the skewers to the preheated air-fryer and air-fry for 2 minutes, then turn the skewers over and cook for a further 2 minutes. Check the internal temperature of the prawns has reached at least 50°C/120°F using a meat thermometer – if not, cook for another few minutes and serve.

Store-cupboard Fishcakes

Servings: 3
Cooking Time:xx

Ingredients:

- 400 g/14 oz. cooked potato – either mashed potato or the insides of jacket potatoes (see page 124)
- 2 x 150–200-g/5½–7-oz. cans fish, such as tuna or salmon, drained
- 2 eggs
- ¾ teaspoon salt
- 1 teaspoon dried parsley
- ½ teaspoon freshly ground black pepper
- 1 tablespoon olive oil
- caper dressing (see page 79), to serve

Directions:

1. Mix the cooked potato, fish, eggs, salt, parsley and pepper together in a bowl, then divide into 6 equal portions and form into fishcakes. Drizzle the olive oil over both sides of each fishcake.
2. Preheat the air-fryer to 180°C/350°F.
3. Add the fishcakes to the preheated air-fryer and air-fry for 15 minutes, turning halfway through cooking. Serve with salad and tartare sauce or Caper Dressing.

Thai-style Tuna Fishcakes

Servings: 2
Cooking Time:xx

Ingredients:

- 200 g/7 oz. cooked potato
- 145 g/5 oz. canned tuna, drained
- 60 g/1 cup canned sweetcorn/corn kernels (drained weight)
- ½ teaspoon soy sauce
- ½ teaspoon fish sauce
- ½ teaspoon Thai 7 spice
- freshly squeezed juice of ½ a lime
- 1 teaspoon freshly grated garlic
- 1 teaspoon freshly grated ginger
- avocado or olive oil, for brushing
- LIME-ALMOND SATAY SAUCE
- 20 ml/4 teaspoons fresh lime juice
- 2 heaped tablespoons almond butter
- 1 teaspoon soy sauce
- ½ teaspoon freshly grated ginger
- ½ teaspoon freshly grated garlic
- ½ teaspoon avocado or olive oil
- ½ teaspoon maple syrup

Directions:

1. Combine all the fishcake ingredients in a food processor and blend together. Divide the mixture into 6 equal portions and mould into fishcakes. Brush a little oil over the top surface of the fishcakes.
2. Preheat the air-fryer to 180°C/350°F.
3. Place the fishcakes on an air-fryer liner or a piece of pierced parchment paper and add to the preheated air-fryer. Air-fry for 4 minutes, then turn over and brush the other side of each fishcake with oil and air-fry for a further 4 minutes.
4. To make the satay dipping sauce, mix all ingredients in a bowl with 1 tablespoon warm water. Serve alongside the fishcakes.

Mahi Fish Tacos

Servings: 4
Cooking Time:xx
Ingredients:

- 400g fresh mahi
- 8 small corn tortillas
- 2 tsp cajun seasoning
- 5 tbsp sour cream
- 2 tbsp mayonnaise
- 2 tbsp scotch bonnet pepper sauce (use 1 tbsp if you don't like your food too spicy)
- 1 tbsp sriracha sauce
- 2 tbsp lime juice
- Salt and pepper to taste
- 1 tbsp vegetable oil

Directions:

1. Clean the mahi. Cut into half inch slices and season with salt
2. Mix quarter parts cayenne pepper and black pepper with cajun seasoning. Sprinkle onto fish
3. Brush pepper sauce on both sides of the fish
4. Set the air fryer to 180°C and cook for about 10 minutes or until golden brown
5. Whilst the fish cooks make the chipotle lime cream. Mix the mayo, sour cream, lime juice sriracha and cayenne pepper
6. Assemble tacos and enjoy

Traditional Fish And Chips

Servings: 4
Cooking Time:xx
Ingredients:

- 4 potatoes, peeled and cut into chips
- 2 fish fillets of your choice
- 1 beaten egg
- 3 slices of wholemeal bread, grated into breadcrumbs
- 25g tortilla crisps
- 1 lemon rind and juice
- 1 tbsp parsley
- Salt and pepper to taste

Directions:

1. Preheat your air fryer to 200°C
2. Place the chips inside and cook until crispy
3. Cut the fish fillets into 4 slices and season with lemon juice
4. Place the breadcrumbs, lemon rind, parsley, tortillas and seasoning into a food processor and blitz to create a crumb consistency
5. Place the breadcrumbs on a large plate
6. Coat the fish in the egg and then the breadcrumb mixture
7. Cook for 15 minutes at 180°C

Peppery Lemon Shrimp

Servings: 2
Cooking Time:xx

Ingredients:

- 300g uncooked shrimp
- 1 tbsp olive oil
- 1 the juice of 1 lemon
- 0.25 tsp garlic powder
- 1 sliced lemon
- 1 tsp pepper
- 0.25 tsp paprika

Directions:

1. Heat the fryer to 200°C
2. Take a medium sized mixing bowl and combine the lemon juice, pepper, garlic powder, paprika and the olive oil together
3. Add the shrimp to the bowl and make sure they're well coated
4. Arrange the shrimp into the basket of the fryer
5. Cook for between 6-8 minutes, until firm and pink

Thai Salmon Patties

Servings: 7
Cooking Time:xx

Ingredients:

- 1 large can of salmon, drained and bones removed
- 30g panko breadcrumbs
- ¼ tsp salt
- 1 ½ tbsp Thai red curry paste
- 1 ½ tbsp brown sugar
- Zest of 1 lime
- 2 eggs
- Cooking spray

Directions:

1. Take a large bowl and combine all ingredients together until smooth
2. Use your hands to create patties that are around 1 inch in thickness
3. Preheat your air fryer to 180°C
4. Coat the patties with cooking spray
5. Cook for 4 minutes each side

Lemon Pepper Shrimp

Servings: 2
Cooking Time:xx
Ingredients:

- ½ tbsp olive oil
- The juice of 1 lemon
- ¼ tsp paprika
- 1 tsp lemon pepper
- ¼ tsp garlic powder
- 400g uncooked shrimp
- 1 sliced lemon

Directions:

1. Preheat air fryer to 200°C
2. Mix olive oil, lemon juice, paprika, lemon pepper and garlic powder. Add the shrimp and mix well
3. Place shrimp in the air fryer and cook for 6-8 minutes until pink and firm.
4. Serve with lemon slices

Beef & Lamb And Pork Recipes

Mongolian Beef

Servings: 4
Cooking Time:xx
Ingredients:

- 500g steak
- 25g cornstarch
- 2 tsp vegetable oil
- ½ tsp ginger
- 1 tbsp garlic minced
- 75g soy sauce
- 75g water
- 100g brown sugar

Directions:

1. Slice the steak and coat in corn starch
2. Place in the air fryer and cook at 200°C for 10 minutes turning halfway
3. Place remaining ingredients in a sauce pan and gently warm
4. When cooked place the steak in a bowl and pour the sauce over

Asian Meatballs

Servings: 2
Cooking Time:xx

Ingredients:

- 500g minced pork
- 2 eggs
- 100g breadcrumbs
- 1 tsp minced garlic
- ⅓ tsp chilli flakes
- 1 tsp minced ginger
- 1 tsp sesame oil
- 1 tsp soy
- 2 diced spring onions
- Salt and pepper to taste

Directions:

1. Mix all ingredients in a bowl until combined
2. Form mix into 1 ½ inch meatballs
3. Place in the air fryer and cook at 200°C for about 10 minutes until cooked

Beef Kebobs

Servings: 4
Cooking Time:xx

Ingredients:

- 500g cubed beef
- 25g low fat sour cream
- 2 tbsp soy sauce
- 8 x 6 inch skewers
- 1 bell pepper
- Half an onion

Directions:

1. Mix the sour cream and soy sauce in a bowl, add the cubed beef and marinate for at least 30 minutes
2. Cut the pepper and onion into 1 inch pieces, soak the skewers in water for 10 minutes
3. Thread beef, bell peppers and onion onto skewers
4. Cook in the air fryer at 200°C for 10 minutes turning halfway

Traditional Empanadas

Servings: 2
Cooking Time:xx
Ingredients:

- 300g minced beef
- 1 tbsp olive oil
- ¼ cup finely chopped onion
- 150g chopped mushrooms
- ⅛ tsp cinnamon
- 4 chopped tomatoes
- 2 tsp chopped garlic
- 6 green olives
- ¼ tsp paprika
- ¼ tsp cumin
- 8 goyoza wrappers
- 1 beaten egg

Directions:

1. Heat oil in a pan add onion and minced beef and cook until browned
2. Add mushrooms and cook for 6 minutes
3. Add garlic, olives, paprika, cumin and cinnamon, and cook for about 3 minutes
4. Stir in tomatoes and cook for 1 minute, set aside allow to cool
5. Place 1 ½ tbsp of filling in each goyoza wrapper
6. Brush edges with egg fold over and seal pinching edges
7. Place in the air fryer and cook at 200 for about 7 minutes

Salt And Pepper Belly Pork

Servings: 4
Cooking Time:xx
Ingredients:

- 500g belly pork
- 1 tsp pepper
- ½ tsp salt

Directions:

1. Cut the pork into bite size pieces and season with salt and pepper
2. Heat the air fryer to 200°C
3. Place in the air fryer and cook for 15 minutes until crisp

Japanese Pork Chops

Servings: 4
Cooking Time:xx

Ingredients:

- 6 boneless pork chops
- 30g flour
- 2 beaten eggs
- 2 tbsp sweet chilli sauce
- 500g cup seasoned breadcrumbs
- ⅛ tsp salt
- ⅛ tsp pepper
- Tonkatsu sauce to taste

Directions:

1. Place the flour, breadcrumbs and eggs in 3 separate bowls
2. Sprinkle both sides of the pork with salt and pepper
3. Coat the pork in flour, egg and then breadcrumbs
4. Place in the air fryer and cook at 180°C for 8 minutes, turn then cook for a further 5 minutes
5. Serve with sauces on the side

Lamb Calzone

Servings: 2
Cooking Time:xx

Ingredients:

- 1 tsp olive oil
- 1 chopped onion
- 100g baby spinach leaves
- 400g minced pork
- 250g whole wheat pizza dough
- 300g grated cheese

Directions:

1. Heat the olive oil in a pan, add the onion and cook for about 2 minutes
2. Add the spinach and cook for a further 1 ½ minutes
3. Stir in marinara sauce and the minced pork
4. Divide the dough into four and roll out into circles
5. Add ¼ of filling to each piece of dough
6. Sprinkle with cheese and fold the dough over to create half moons, crimp edges to seal
7. Spray with cooking spray, place in the air fryer and cook at 160°C for 12 minutes turning after 8 minutes

Fillet Mignon Wrapped In Bacon

Servings: 2
Cooking Time:xx
Ingredients:

- 1 kg filet mignon
- 500g bacon slices
- Olive oil

Directions:

1. Wrap the fillets in bacon
2. Season with salt and pepper and brush with olive oil
3. Place in the air fryer cook at 200°C for 9 minutes turning halfway through

Hamburgers With Feta

Servings: 4
Cooking Time:xx
Ingredients:

- 400g minced beef
- 250g crumbled feta
- 25g chopped green olives
- ½ tsp garlic powder
- ½ cup chopped onion
- 2 tbsp Worcestershire sauce
- ½ tsp steak seasoning
- Salt to taste

Directions:

1. Mix all the ingredients in a bowl
2. Divide the mix into four and shape into patties
3. Place in the air fryer and cook at 200°C for about 15 minutes

Sausage Burritos

Servings:4
Cooking Time:20 Minutes

Ingredients:

- 1 medium sweet potato
- 2 tbsp olive oil
- 1 tsp salt
- 1 tsp black pepper
- 8 sausages, uncooked
- 4 white flour tortillas
- 4 eggs, beaten
- 200 ml milk (any kind)
- 100 g / 3.5 oz cheddar cheese, grated

Directions:

1. Preheat the air fryer to 200 °C / 400 °F and line the air fryer mesh basket with parchment paper.
2. Peel the sweet potato and cut it into small chunks.
3. Place the sweet potato chunks in a bowl and toss in 1 tbsp olive oil. Sprinkle salt and pepper over the top.
4. Transfer the sweet potato chunks into the air fryer and cook for 8-10 minutes until hot. Remove from the air fryer and set aside to drain on paper towels.
5. Heat 1 tbsp olive oil in a medium frying pan and cook the sausages for 5-7 minutes until slightly browned. Remove the sausages and set them aside on paper towels to drain.
6. In a bowl, whisk together the beaten eggs and milk, and pour into the hot frying pan. Cook the eggs and use a fork to scramble them as they cook in the pan.
7. Once the eggs are cooked, mix them with the potatoes, sausages, and cheddar cheese in a bowl.
8. Spread the mixture evenly across the 4 white flour tortillas and roll them each up into tight burritos. Use a toothpick to keep them together if necessary.
9. Place the burritos into the hot air fryer and cook for 6-8 minutes, turning them over halfway through.
10. Enjoy the burritos for breakfast or lunch.

Tahini Beef Bites

Servings: 2
Cooking Time:xx

Ingredients:

- 500g sirloin steak, cut into cubes
- 2 tbsp Za'atar seasoning
- 1 tsp olive oil
- 25g Tahini
- 25g warm water
- 1 tbsp lemon juice
- 1 clove of garlic
- Salt to taste

Directions:

1. Preheat the air fryer to 250°C
2. Take a bowl and combine the oil with the steak, salt, and Za'atar seasoning
3. Place in the air fryer and cook for 10 minutes, turning halfway through
4. Take a bowl and combine the water, garlic, lemon juice, salt, and tahini, or use a food processor if you have one
5. Pour the sauce over the bites and serve

Taco Lasagne Pie

Servings: 4
Cooking Time:xx
Ingredients:

- 450g ground beef
- 2 tbsp olive oil
- 1 chopped onion
- 1 minced garlic clove
- 1 tsp cumin
- 1 tsp oregano
- 1/2 tsp adobo
- 266g grated Cheddar cheese
- 4 flour tortillas
- 112g tomato sauce

Directions:

1. Soften the onions with the olive oil in a frying pan
2. Add the beef and garlic until the meat has browned
3. Add the tomato sauce, cumin, oregano, and adobo and combine
4. Allow to simmer for a few minutes
5. Place one tortilla on the bottom of your air fryer basket
6. Add a meat layer, followed by a layer of the cheese, and continue alternating this routine until you have no meat left
7. Add a tortilla on top and sprinkle with the rest of the cheese
8. Cook at 180°C for 8 minutes

Meatballs In Tomato Sauce

Servings: 4
Cooking Time:xx
Ingredients:

- 1 small onion
- 300g minced pork
- 1 tbsp chopped parsley
- 1 tbsp thyme
- 1 egg
- 3 tbsp bread crumbs
- Salt and pepper to taste

Directions:

1. Place all ingredients into a bowl and mix well
2. Shape mixture into 12 meatballs
3. Heat the air fryer to 200°C
4. Place the meatballs into the air fryer and cook for about 7 minutes
5. Tip the meatballs into an oven dish add the tomato sauce and cook for about 5 minutes in the air fryer until warmed through

Steak And Mushrooms

Servings: 4
Cooking Time:xx
Ingredients:

- 500g cubed sirloin steak
- 300g button mushrooms
- 3 tbsp Worcestershire sauce
- 1 tbsp olive oil
- 1 tsp parsley flakes
- 1 tsp paprika
- 1 tsp crushed chilli flakes

Directions:

1. Combine all ingredients in a bowl, cover and chill for at least 4 hours
2. Preheat air fryer to 200°C
3. Drain and discard the marinade from the steak
4. Place the steak and mushrooms in the air fryer and cook for 5 minutes
5. Toss and cook for a further 5 minutes

Pork Belly With Crackling

Servings: 4
Cooking Time:xx
Ingredients:

- 800g belly pork
- 1 tsp sea salt
- 1 tsp garlic salt
- 2 tsp five spice
- 1 tsp rosemary
- 1 tsp white pepper
- 1 tsp sugar
- Half a lemon

Directions:

1. Cut lines into the meat portion of the belly pork
2. Cook thoroughly in water
3. Allow to air dry for 3 hours
4. Score the skin and prick holes with a fork
5. Rub with the dry rub mix, rub some lemon juice on the skin
6. Place in the air fryer and cook at 160°C for 30 minutes then at 180°C for a further 30 minutes

Roast Pork

Servings: 4
Cooking Time:xx
Ingredients:

- 500g pork joint
- 1 tbsp olive oil
- 1 tsp salt

Directions:

1. Preheat air fryer to 180°C
2. Score the pork skin with a knife
3. Drizzle the pork with oil and rub it into the skin, sprinkle with salt
4. Place in the air fryer and cook for about 50 minutes

Chinese Pork With Pineapple

Servings: 4
Cooking Time:xx
Ingredients:

- 450g pork loin, cubed
- ½ tsp salt
- ½ tsp pepper
- 1 tbsp brown sugar
- 75g fresh coriander, chopped
- 2 tbsp toasted sesame seeds
- ½ pineapple, cubed
- 1 sliced red pepper
- 1 minced clove of garlic
- 1 tsp ginger
- 2 tbsp soy
- 1 tbsp oil

Directions:

1. Season the pork with salt and pepper
2. Add all ingredients to the air fryer
3. Cook at 180°C for 17 minutes
4. Serve and garnish with coriander and toasted sesame seeds

Char Siu Buffalo

Servings: 2
Cooking Time:xx

Ingredients:

- 1 kg beef, cut into strips
- 4 tbsp honey
- 2 tbsp sugar
- 2 tbsp char siu sauce
- 2 tbsp oyster sauce
- 2 tbsp soy sauce
- 2 tbsp olive oil
- 2 tsp minced garlic
- ¼ tsp bi carbonate of soda

Directions:

1. Place all the ingredients in a bowl, mix well and marinate over night
2. Line the air fryer with foil, add the beef, keep the marinade to one side
3. Cook at 200°C for 10 minutes
4. Brush the pork with the sauce and cook for another 20 minutes at 160°C
5. Remove the meat and set aside
6. Strain the marinade into a saucepan, heat until it thickens
7. Drizzle over the pork and serve with rice

Pork Chops With Raspberry And Balsamic

Servings: 4
Cooking Time:xx

Ingredients:

- 2 large eggs
- 30ml milk
- 250g panko bread crumbs
- 250g finely chopped pecans
- 1 tbsp orange juice
- 4 pork chops
- 30ml balsamic vinegar
- 2 tbsp brown sugar
- 2 tbsp raspberry jam

Directions:

1. Preheat air fryer to 200°C
2. Mix the eggs and milk together in a bowl
3. In another bowl mix the breadcrumbs and pecans
4. Coat the pork chops in flour, egg and then coat in the breadcrumbs
5. Place in the air fryer and cook for 12 minutes until golden turning halfway
6. Put the remaining ingredients in a pan simmer for about 6 minutes, serve with the pork chops

Pork Chilli Cheese Dogs

Servings: 2
Cooking Time:xx
Ingredients:

- 1 can of pork chilli, or chilli you have left over
- 200g grated cheese
- 2 hot dog bread rolls
- 2 hot dogs

Directions:

1. Preheat the air fryer to 260°C
2. Cook the hot dogs for 4 minutes, turning halfway
3. Place the hotdogs inside the bread rolls and place back inside the air fryer
4. Top with half the cheese on top and then the chilli
5. Add the rest of the cheese
6. Cook for an extra 2 minutes

Chinese Chilli Beef

Servings: 2
Cooking Time:xx
Ingredients:

- 4 tbsp light soy sauce
- 1 tsp honey
- 3 tbsp tomato ketchup
- 1 tsp Chinese 5 spice
- 1 tbsp oil
- 6 tbsp sweet chilli sauce
- 1 tbsp lemon juice
- 400g frying steak
- 2 tbsp cornflour

Directions:

1. Slice the steak into strips, put into a bowl and cover with cornflour and 5 spice
2. Add to the air fryer and cook for 6 minutes at 200°C
3. Whilst the beef is cooking mix together the remaining ingredients
4. Add to the air fryer and cook for another 3 minutes

Beef Bulgogi Burgers

Servings: 4
Cooking Time:xx

Ingredients:

- 500g minced beef
- 2 tbsp gochujang
- 1 tbsp soy
- 2 tsp minced garlic
- 2 tsp minced ginger
- 2 tsp sugar
- 1 tbsp olive oil
- 1 chopped onion

Directions:

1. Mix all the ingredients in a large bowl, allow to rest for at least 30 minutes in the fridge
2. Divide the meat into four and form into patties
3. Place in the air fryer and cook at 180°C for about 10 minutes
4. Serve in burger buns, if desired

Poultry Recipes

Bbq Chicken Tenders

Servings: 6
Cooking Time:xx

Ingredients:

- 300g barbecue flavoured pork rinds
- 200g all purpose flour
- 1 tbsp barbecue seasoning
- 1 egg
- 400g chicken breast tenderloins
- Cooking spray

Directions:

1. Preheat the air fryer to 190°C
2. Place the pork rinds into a food processor and blitz to a breadcrumb consistency, before transferring to a bowl
3. In a separate bowl, combine the flour and barbecue seasoning
4. Beat the egg in a small bowl
5. Take the chicken and first dip into the egg, then the flour, and then the breadcrumbs
6. Place the chicken into the air fryer and spray with cooking spray and cook for about 15 minutes

Honey Cajun Chicken Thighs

Servings: 6
Cooking Time:xx

Ingredients:

- 100ml buttermilk
- 1 tsp hot sauce
- 400g skinless, boneless chicken thighs
- 150g all purpose flour
- 60g tapioca flour
- 2.5 tsp cajun seasoning
- ½ tsp garlic salt
- ½ tsp honey powder
- ¼ tsp ground paprika
- ⅛ tsp cayenne pepper
- 4 tsp honey

Directions:

1. Take a large bowl and combine the buttermilk and hot sauce
2. Transfer to a plastic bag and add the chicken thighs
3. Allow to marinate for 30 minutes
4. Take another bowl and add the flour, tapioca flour, cajun seasoning, garlic, salt, honey powder, paprika, and cayenne pepper, combining well
5. Dredge the chicken through the mixture
6. Preheat the air fryer to 175C
7. Cook for 15 minutes before flipping the thighs over and cooking for another 10 minutes
8. Drizzle 1 tsp of honey over each thigh

Chicken Fried Rice

Servings: 4
Cooking Time:xx

Ingredients:

- 400g cooked white rice
- 400g cooked chicken, diced
- 200g frozen peas and carrots
- 6 tbsp soy sauce
- 1 tbsp vegetable oil
- 1 diced onion

Directions:

1. Take a large bowl and add the rice, vegetable oil and soy sauce and combine well
2. Add the frozen peas, carrots, diced onion and the chicken and mix together well
3. Pour the mixture into a nonstick pan
4. Place the pan into the air fryer
5. Cook at 182C for 20 minutes

Chicken Tikka

Servings: 2
Cooking Time:xx

Ingredients:

- 2 chicken breasts, diced
- FIRST MARINADE
- freshly squeezed juice of ½ a lemon
- 1 tablespoon freshly grated ginger
- 1 tablespoon freshly grated garlic
- a good pinch of salt
- SECOND MARINADE
- 100 g/½ cup Greek yogurt
- ½ teaspoon chilli powder
- ½ teaspoon chilli paste
- ½ teaspoon turmeric
- ½ teaspoon garam masala
- 1 tablespoon olive oil

Directions:

1. Mix the ingredients for the first marinade together in a bowl, add in the chicken and stir to coat all the chicken pieces. Leave in the fridge to marinate for 20 minutes.
2. Combine the second marinade ingredients. Once the first marinade has had 20 minutes, add the second marinade to the chicken and stir well. Leave in the fridge for at least 4 hours.
3. Preheat the air-fryer to 180°C/350°F.
4. Thread the chicken pieces onto metal skewers that fit in your air-fryer. Add the skewers to the preheated air-fryer and air-fry for 10 minutes. Check the internal temperature of the chicken has reached at least 74°C/165°F using a meat thermometer – if not, cook for another few minutes and then serve.

Whole Chicken

Servings: 4
Cooking Time:xx

Ingredients:

- 1.5-kg/3¼-lb. chicken
- 2 tablespoons butter or coconut oil
- salt and freshly ground black pepper

Directions:

1. Place the chicken breast-side up and carefully insert the butter or oil between the skin and the flesh of each breast. Season.
2. Preheat the air-fryer to 180°C/350°F. If the chicken hits the heating element, remove the drawer to lower the chicken a level.
3. Add the chicken to the preheated air-fryer breast-side up. Air-fry for 30 minutes, then turn over and cook for a further 10 minutes. Check the internal temperature with a meat thermometer. If it is 75°C/167°F at the thickest part, remove the chicken from the air-fryer and leave to rest for 10 minutes before carving. If less than 75°C/167°F, continue to cook until this internal temperature is reached and then allow to rest.

Healthy Bang Bang Chicken

Servings: 4
Cooking Time:xx
Ingredients:

- 500g chicken breasts, cut into pieces of around 1" in size
- 1 beaten egg
- 50ml milk
- 1 tbsp hot pepper sauce
- 80g flour
- 70g tapioca starch
- 1 ½ tsp seasoned starch
- 1 tsp garlic granules
- ½ tsp cumin
- 6 tbsp plain Greek yogurt
- 3 tbsp sweet chilli sauce
- 1 tsp hot sauce

Directions:

1. Preheat the air fryer to 190°C
2. Take a mixing bowl and combine the egg, milk and hot sauce
3. Take another bowl and combine the flour, tapioca starch, salt, garlic and cumin
4. Dip the chicken pieces into the sauce bowl and then into the flour bowl
5. Place the chicken into the air fryer
6. Whilst cooking, mix together the Greek yogurt, sweet chilli sauce and hot sauce and serve with the chicken

Charred Chicken Breasts

Servings: 2
Cooking Time:xx
Ingredients:

- 2 tsp paprika
- 1 tsp ground thyme
- 1 tsp cumin
- ½ tsp cayenne pepper
- ½ tsp onion powder
- ½ tsp black pepper
- ¼ tsp salt
- 2 tsp vegetable oil
- 2 skinless boneless chicken breasts, cut into halves

Directions:

1. Take a bowl and add the paprika, thyme, cumin, cayenne pepper, onion powder, black pepper and salt
2. Coat each chicken breast with oil and dredge chicken in the spice mixture
3. Preheat air fryer to 175C
4. Cook for 10 minutes and flip
5. Cook for 10 more minutes

Air Fried Maple Chicken Thighs

Servings: 4
Cooking Time:xx

Ingredients:

- 200ml buttermilk
- ½ tbsp maple syrup
- 1 egg
- 1 tsp granulated garlic salt
- 4 chicken thighs with the bone in
- 140g all purpose flour
- 65g tapioca flour
- 1 tsp sweet paprika
- 1 tsp onion powder
- ¼ tsp ground black pepper
- ¼ tsp cayenne pepper
- ½ tsp granulated garlic
- ½ tsp honey powder

Directions:

1. Take a bowl and combine the buttermilk, maple syrup, egg and garlic powder
2. Transfer to a bag and add chicken thighs, shaking to combine well
3. Set aside for 1 hour
4. Take a shallow bowl and add the flour, tapioca flour, salt, sweet paprika, smoked paprika, pepper, cayenne pepper and honey powder, combining well
5. Preheat the air fryer to 190°C
6. Drag the chicken through flour mixture and place the chicken skin side down in the air fryer Cook for 12 minutes, until white in the middle

Grain-free Chicken Katsu

Servings: 4
Cooking Time:xx

Ingredients:

- 125 g/1¼ cups ground almonds
- ½ teaspoon salt
- ½ teaspoon garlic powder
- ½ teaspoon dried parsley
- ½ teaspoon freshly ground black pepper
- ¼ teaspoon onion powder
- ¼ teaspoon dried oregano
- 450 g/1 lb. mini chicken fillets
- 1 egg, beaten
- oil, for spraying/drizzling
- coriander/cilantro leaves, to serve
- KATSU SAUCE
- 1 teaspoon olive oil or avocado oil
- 1 courgette/zucchini (approx. 150 g/5 oz.), finely chopped
- 1 carrot (approx. 100 g/3½ oz.), finely chopped
- 1 onion (approx. 120 g/4½ oz.), finely chopped
- 1 eating apple (approx. 150 g/5 oz.), cored and finely chopped
- 1 teaspoon ground ginger
- 1 teaspoon ground turmeric
- 2 teaspoons ground cumin
- 2 teaspoons ground coriander
- 1½ teaspoons mild chilli/chili powder
- 1 teaspoon garlic powder
- 1½ tablespoons runny honey
- 1 tablespoon soy sauce (gluten-free if you wish)
- 700 ml/3 cups vegetable stock (700 ml/3 cups water with 1½ stock cubes)

Directions:

1. First make the sauce. The easiest way to ensure all the vegetables and apple are finely chopped is to combine them in a food processor. Heat the oil in a large saucepan and sauté the finely chopped vegetables and apple for 5 minutes. Add all the seasonings, honey, soy sauce and stock and stir well, then bring to a simmer and simmer for 30 minutes.
2. Meanwhile, mix together the ground almonds, seasonings and spices. Dip each chicken fillet into the beaten egg, then into the almond-spice mix, making sure each fillet is fully coated. Spray the coated chicken fillets with olive oil (or simply drizzle over).
3. Preheat the air-fryer to 180°C/350°F.
4. Place the chicken fillets in the preheated air-fryer and air-fry for 10 minutes, turning halfway through cooking. Check the internal temperature of the chicken has reached at least 74°C/165°F using a meat thermometer – if not, cook for another few minutes.
5. Blend the cooked sauce in a food processor until smooth. Serve the chicken with the Katsu Sauce drizzled over (if necessary, reheat the sauce gently before serving) and scattered with coriander leaves. Any unused sauce can be frozen.

Chicken And Cheese Chimichangas

Servings: 6
Cooking Time:xx
Ingredients:

- 100g shredded chicken (cooked)
- 150g nacho cheese
- 1 chopped jalapeño pepper
- 6 flour tortillas
- 5 tbsp salsa
- 60g refried beans
- 1 tsp cumin
- 0.5 tsp chill powder
- Salt and pepper to taste

Directions:

1. Take a large mixing bowl and add all of the ingredients, combining well
2. Add ⅓ of the filling to each tortilla and roll into a burrito shape
3. Spray the air fryer with cooking spray and heat to 200°C
4. Place the chimichangas in the air fryer and cook for 7 minutes

Turkey Cutlets In Mushroom Sauce

Servings: 2
Cooking Time:xx
Ingredients:

- 2 turkey cutlets
- 1 tbsp butter
- 1 can of cream of mushroom sauce
- 160ml milk
- Salt and pepper for seasoning

Directions:

1. Preheat the air fryer to 220°C
2. Brush the turkey cults with the butter and seasoning
3. Place in the air fryer and cook for 11 minutes
4. Add the mushroom soup and milk to a pan and cook over the stone for around 10 minutes, stirring every so often
5. Top the turkey cutlets with the sauce

Quick Chicken Nuggets

Servings: 4
Cooking Time:xx

Ingredients:

- 500g chicken tenders
- 25g ranch salad dressing mixture
- 2 tbsp plain flour
- 100g breadcrumbs
- 1 egg, beaten
- Olive oil spray

Directions:

1. Take a large mixing bowl and arrange the chicken inside
2. Sprinkle the seasoning over the top and ensure the chicken is evenly coated
3. Place the chicken to one side for around 10 minutes
4. Add the flour into a resealable bag
5. Crack the egg into a small mixing bowl and whisk
6. Pour the breadcrumbs onto a medium sized plate
7. Transfer the chicken into the resealable bag and coat with the flour, giving it a good shake
8. Remove the chicken and dip into the egg, and then rolling it into the breadcrumbs, coating evenly
9. Repeat with all pieces of the chicken
10. Heat your air fryer to 200°C
11. Arrange the chicken inside the fryer and add a little olive oil spray to avoid sticking
12. Cook for 4 minutes, before turning over and cooking for another 4 minutes
13. Remove and serve whilst hot

Thai Turkey Burgers

Servings: 4
Cooking Time:xx

Ingredients:

- 1 courgette/zucchini, about 200 g/7 oz.
- 400 g/14 oz. minced/ground turkey breast
- 35 g/½ cup fresh breadcrumbs (gluten-free if you wish)
- 1 teaspoon Thai 7 spice seasoning
- 1 teaspoon salt
- 1 teaspoon olive oil

Directions:

1. Coarsely grate the courgette/zucchini, then place in a piece of muslin/cheesecloth and squeeze out the water. Combine the grated courgette with all other ingredients except the olive oil, mixing together well. Divide the mixture into 4 equal portions and mould into burgers. Brush with oil.
2. Preheat the air-fryer to 190°C/375°C.
3. Add the turkey burgers to the preheated air-fryer and air-fry for 15 minutes, turning once halfway through cooking. Check the internal temperature of the burgers has reached at least 74°C/165°F using a meat thermometer – if not, cook for another few minutes and then serve.

Olive Stained Turkey Breast

Servings: 14
Cooking Time:xx

Ingredients:

- The brine from a can of olives
- 150ml buttermilk
- 300g boneless and skinless turkey breasts
- 1 sprig fresh rosemary
- 2 sprigs fresh thyme

Directions:

1. Take a mixing bowl and combine the olive brine and buttermilk
2. Pour the mixture over the turkey breast
3. Add the rosemary and thyme sprigs
4. Place into the refrigerator for 8 hours
5. Remove from the fridge and let the turkey reach room temperature
6. Preheat the air fryer to 175C
7. Cook for 15 minutes, ensuring the turkey is cooked through before serving

Chicken Fajitas

Servings: 3
Cooking Time:xx

Ingredients:

- 2 boneless chicken breasts, sliced into strips
- 5 mini (bell) peppers, sliced into strips
- 1 courgette/zucchini, sliced into 5-mm/¼-in. thick discs
- 2 tablespoons olive oil
- 28-g/1-oz. packet fajita seasoning mix
- TO SERVE
- wraps
- sliced avocado
- chopped tomato and red onion
- grated Red Leicester cheese
- plain yogurt
- coriander/cilantro
- lime wedges, for squeezing

Directions:

1. Combine the chicken, (bell) peppers, courgettes/zucchini and olive oil in a bowl. Add the fajita seasoning and stir to coat.
2. Preheat the air-fryer to 180°C/350°F.
3. Add the coated vegetables and chicken to the preheated air-fryer and air-fry for 12 minutes, shaking the drawer a couple of times during cooking. Check the internal temperature of the chicken has reached at least 74°C/165°F using a meat thermometer – if not, cook for another few minutes.
4. Serve immediately alongside the serving suggestions or your own choices of accompaniments.

Hawaiian Chicken

Servings: 2
Cooking Time:xx

Ingredients:

- 2 chicken breasts
- 1 tbsp butter
- A pinch of salt and pepper
- 160ml pineapple juice
- 25g brown sugar
- 3 tbsp soy sauce
- 2 tsp water
- 1 clove of garlic, minced
- 1 tsp grated ginger
- 2 tsp cornstarch

Directions:

1. Preheat the air fryer to 260°C
2. Take a bowl and combine the butter and salt and pepper
3. Cover the chicken with the butter and cook in the fryer for 15 minutes, turning halfway
4. Remove and allow to rest for 5 minutes
5. Take another bowl and mix together the pineapple juice, soy sauce, garlic, ginger, and brown sugar
6. Transfer to a saucepan and simmer for 5 minutes
7. Combine the water and cornstarch and add to the sauce, stirring continually for another minute
8. Slice the chicken into strips and pour the sauce over the top

Air Fryer Bbq Chicken

Servings: 4
Cooking Time:xx

Ingredients:

- 1 whole chicken
- 2 tbsp avocado oil
- 1 tbsp kosher salt
- 1 tsp ground pepper
- 1 tsp garlic powder
- 1 tsp paprika
- ½ tsp dried basil
- ½ tsp dried oregano
- ½ tsp dried thyme

Directions:

1. Mix the seasonings together and spread over chicken
2. Place the chicken in the air fryer breast side down
3. Cook at 182C for 50 minutes and then breast side up for 10 minutes
4. Carve and serve

Chicken Parmesan With Marinara Sauce

Servings: 4
Cooking Time:xx
Ingredients:

- 400g chicken breasts, sliced in half
- 250g panko breadcrumbs
- 140g grated parmesan cheese
- 140g grated mozzarella cheese
- 3 egg whites
- 200g marinara sauce
- 2 tsp Italian seasoning
- Salt and pepper to taste
- Cooking spray

Directions:

1. Preheat the air fryer to 200°C
2. Lay the chicken slices on the work surface and pound with a mallet or a rolling pin to flatten
3. Take a mixing bowl and add the panko breadcrumbs, cheese and the seasoning, combining well
4. Add the egg whites into a separate bowl
5. Dip the chicken into the egg whites and then the breadcrumbs
6. Cook for 7 minutes in the air fryer

Cheddar & Bbq Stuffed Chicken

Servings: 2
Cooking Time:xx
Ingredients:

- 3 strips of bacon
- 100g cheddar cheese
- 3 tbsp barbecue sauce
- 300g skinless and boneless chicken breasts
- salt and ground pepper to taste

Directions:

1. Preheat the air fryer to 190°C
2. Cook one of the back strips for 2 minutes, before cutting into small pieces
3. Increase the temperature of the air fryer to 200°C
4. Mix together the cooked bacon, cheddar cheese and 1 tbsp barbecue sauce
5. Take the chicken and make a pouch by cutting a 1 inch gap into the top
6. Stuff the pouch with the bacon and cheese mixture and then wrap around the chicken breast
7. Coat the chicken with the rest of the BBQ sauce
8. Cook for 10 minutes in the air fryer, before turning and cooking for an additional 10 minutes

Buffalo Wings

Servings: 4
Cooking Time:xx
Ingredients:

- 500g chicken wings
- 1 tbsp olive oil
- 5 tbsp cayenne pepper sauce
- 75g butter
- 2 tbsp vinegar
- 1 tsp garlic powder
- ¼ tsp cayenne pepper

Directions:

1. Preheat the air fryer to 182C
2. Take a large mixing bowl and add the chicken wings
3. Drizzle oil over the wings, coating evenly
4. Cook for 25 minutes and then flip the wings and cook for 5 more minutes
5. In a saucepan over a medium heat, mix the hot pepper sauce, butter, vinegar, garlic powder and cayenne pepper, combining well
6. Pour the sauce over the wings and flip to coat, before serving

Buttermilk Chicken

Servings: 4
Cooking Time:xx
Ingredients:

- 500g chicken thighs, skinless and boneless
- 180ml buttermilk
- 40g tapioca flour
- ½ tsp garlic salt
- 1 egg
- 75g all purpose flour
- ½ tsp brown sugar
- 1 tsp garlic powder
- ½ tsp paprika
- ½ tsp onion powder
- ¼ tsp oregano
- Salt and pepper to taste

Directions:

1. Take a medium mixing bowl and combine the buttermilk and hot sauce
2. Add the tapioca flour, garlic salt and black pepper in a plastic bag and shake
3. Beat the egg
4. Take the chicken thighs and tip into the buttermilk, then the tapioca mixture, the egg, and then the flour
5. Preheat air fryer to 190°C
6. Cook the chicken thighs for 10 minutes, until white in the middle

Pizza Chicken Nuggets

Servings: 2
Cooking Time:xx
Ingredients:

- 60 g/¾ cup dried breadcrumbs (see page 9)
- 20 g/¼ cup grated Parmesan
- ½ teaspoon dried oregano
- ¼ teaspoon freshly ground black pepper
- 150 g/⅔ cup Mediterranean sauce (see page 102) or 150 g/5½ oz. jarred tomato pasta sauce (keep any leftover sauce for serving)
- 400 g/14 oz. chicken fillets

Directions:

1. Preheat the air-fryer to 180°C/350°F.
2. Combine the breadcrumbs, Parmesan, oregano and pepper in a bowl. Have the Mediterranean or pasta sauce in a separate bowl.
3. Dip each chicken fillet in the tomato sauce first, then roll in the breadcrumb mix until coated fully.
4. Add the breaded fillets to the preheated air-fryer and air-fry for 10 minutes. Check the internal temperature of the chicken has reached at least 74°C/165°F using a meat thermometer – if not, cook for another few minutes.
5. Serve with some additional sauce that has been warmed through.

Side Dishes Recipes

Butternut Squash

Servings: 4
Cooking Time:xx
Ingredients:

- 500 g/1 lb. 2 oz. butternut squash, chopped into 2.5-cm/1-in. cubes
- 1 tablespoon olive oil or avocado oil
- 1 teaspoon smoked paprika
- 1 teaspoon dried oregano
- ½ teaspoon salt
- ¼ teaspoon freshly ground black pepper

Directions:

1. Preheat the air-fryer to 180°C/350°F.
2. In a bowl toss the butternut squash cubes in the oil and all the seasonings.
3. Add the butternut squash cubes to the preheated air-fryer and air-fry for 16–18 minutes, shaking the drawer once during cooking.

Homemade Croquettes

Servings:4
Cooking Time:15 Minutes
Ingredients:

- 400 g / 14 oz white rice, uncooked
- 1 onion, sliced
- 2 cloves garlic, finely sliced
- 2 eggs, beaten
- 50 g / 3.5 oz parmesan cheese, grated
- 1 tsp salt
- 1 tsp black pepper
- 50 g / 3.5 oz breadcrumbs
- 1 tsp dried oregano

Directions:

1. In a large mixing bowl, combine the white rice, onion slices, garlic cloves slices, one beaten egg, parmesan cheese, and a sprinkle of salt and pepper.
2. Whisk the second egg in a separate bowl and place the breadcrumbs into another bowl.
3. Shape the mixture into 12 even croquettes and roll evenly in the egg, followed by the breadcrumbs.
4. Preheat the air fryer to 190 °C / 375 °F and line the bottom of the basket with parchment paper.
5. Place the croquettes in the lined air fryer basket and cook for 15 minutes, turning halfway through, until crispy and golden. Enjoy while hot as a side to your main dish.

Tex Mex Hash Browns

Servings: 4
Cooking Time:xx
Ingredients:

- 500g potatoes cut into cubes
- 1 tbsp olive oil
- 1 red pepper
- 1 onion
- 1 jalapeño pepper
- ½ tsp taco seasoning
- ½ tsp cumin
- Salt and pepper to taste

Directions:

1. Soak the potatoes in water for 20 minutes
2. Heat the air fryer to 160°C
3. Drain the potatoes and coat with olive oil
4. Add to the air fryer and cook for 18 minutes
5. Mix the remaining ingredients in a bowl, add the potatoes and mix well
6. Place the mix into the air fryer cook for 6 minutes, shake and cook for a further 5 minutes

Orange Sesame Cauliflower

Servings: 4
Cooking Time:xx
Ingredients:

- 100ml water
- 30g cornstarch
- 50g flour
- 1/2 tsp salt
- ½ tsp pepper
- 2 tbsp tomato ketchup
- 2 tbsp brown sugar
- 1 sliced onion

Directions:

1. Mix together flour, cornstarch, water, salt and pepper until smooth
2. Coat the cauliflower and chill for 30 minutes
3. Place in the air fryer and cook for 22 minutes at 170°C
4. Meanwhile combine remaining ingredients in a saucepan, gently simmer until thickened.
5. Mix cauliflower with sauce and top with toasted sesame seeds to serve

Crispy Broccoli

Servings: 2
Cooking Time:xx
Ingredients:

- 170 g/6 oz. broccoli florets
- 2 tablespoons olive oil
- ⅛ teaspoon garlic salt
- ⅛ teaspoon freshly ground black pepper
- 2 tablespoons freshly grated Parmesan or Pecorino

Directions:

1. Preheat the air-fryer to 200°C/400°F.
2. Toss the broccoli in the oil, season with the garlic salt and pepper, then toss over the grated cheese and combine well. Add the broccoli to the preheated air-fryer and air-fry for 5 minutes, giving the broccoli a stir halfway through to ensure even cooking.

Courgette Gratin

Servings: 2
Cooking Time:xx

Ingredients:

- 2 courgette
- 1 tbsp chopped parsley
- 2 tbsp breadcrumbs
- 4 tbsp grated parmesan
- 1 tbsp vegetable oil
- Salt and pepper to taste

Directions:

1. Heat the air fryer to 180°C
2. Cut each courgette in half length ways then slice
3. Mix the remaining ingredients together
4. Place the courgette in the air fryer and top with the breadcrumb mix
5. Cook for about 15 minutes until golden brown

Cauliflower With Hot Sauce And Blue Cheese Sauce

Servings:2
Cooking Time:15 Minutes

Ingredients:

- For the cauliflower:
- 1 cauliflower, broken into florets
- 4 tbsp hot sauce
- 2 tbsp olive oil
- 1 tsp garlic powder
- ½ tsp salt
- ½ tsp black pepper
- 1 tbsp plain flour
- 1 tbsp corn starch
- For the blue cheese sauce:
- 50 g / 1.8 oz blue cheese, crumbled
- 2 tbsp sour cream
- 2 tbsp mayonnaise
- ½ tsp salt
- ½ tsp black pepper

Directions:

1. Preheat the air fryer to 180 °C / 350 °F and line the bottom of the basket with parchment paper.
2. In a bowl, combine the hot sauce, olive oil, garlic powder, salt, and black pepper until it forms a consistent mixture. Add the cauliflower to the bowl and coat in the sauce.
3. Stir in the plain flour and corn starch until well combined.
4. Transfer the cauliflower to the lined basket in the air fryer, close the lid, and cook for 12-15 minutes until the cauliflower has softened and is golden in colour.
5. Meanwhile, make the blue cheese sauce by combining all of the ingredients. When the cauliflower is ready, remove it from the air fryer and serve with the blue cheese sauce on the side.

Aubergine Parmesan

Servings: 4
Cooking Time:xx
Ingredients:

- 100g Italian breadcrumbs
- 50g grated parmesan
- 1 tsp Italian seasoning
- 1 tsp salt
- ½ tsp dried basil
- ½ tsp onion powder
- ½ tsp black pepper
- 100g flour
- 2 eggs
- 1 aubergine, sliced into ½ inch rounds

Directions:

1. Mix breadcrumbs, parmesan, salt Italian seasoning, basil, onion powder and pepper in a bowl
2. Add the flour to another bowl, and beat the eggs in another
3. Dip the aubergine in the flour, then the eggs and then coat in the bread crumbs
4. Preheat the air fryer to 185°C
5. Place the aubergine in the air fryer and cook for 8-10 minutes
6. Turnover and cook for a further 4-6 minutes

Roasted Okra

Servings: 1
Cooking Time:xx
Ingredients:

- 300g Okra, ends trimmed and pods sliced
- 1 tsp olive oil
- ¼ tsp salt
- ⅛ tsp pepper

Directions:

1. Preheat the air fryer to 175°C
2. Combine all ingredients in a bowl and stir gently
3. Place in the air fryer and cook for 5 minutes, shake and cook for another 5 minutes

Asparagus Spears

Servings: 2
Cooking Time:xx

Ingredients:

- 1 bunch of trimmed asparagus
- 1 teaspoon olive oil
- ¼ teaspoon salt
- ⅛ teaspoon freshly ground black pepper

Directions:

1. Preheat the air-fryer to 180°C/350°F.
2. Toss the asparagus spears in the oil and seasoning. Add these to the preheated air-fryer and air-fry for 8–12 minutes, turning once (cooking time depends on the thickness of the stalks, which should retain some bite).

Alternative Stuffed Potatoes

Servings: 4
Cooking Time:xx

Ingredients:

- 4 baking potatoes, peeled and halved
- 1 tbsp olive oil
- 150g grated cheese
- ½ onion, diced
- 2 slices bacon

Directions:

1. Preheat air fryer to 175°C
2. Brush the potatoes with oil and cook in the air fryer for 10 minutes
3. Coat again with oil and cook for a further 10 minutes
4. Cut the potatoes in half spoon the insides into a bowl and mix in the cheese
5. Place the bacon and onion in a pan and cook until browned, mix in with the potato
6. Stuff the skins with the mix and return to the air fryer, cook for about 6 minutes

Potato Wedges With Rosemary

Servings: 2
Cooking Time:xx
Ingredients:

- 2 potatoes, sliced into wedges
- 1 tbsp olive oil
- 2 tsp seasoned salt
- 2 tbsp chopped rosemary

Directions:

1. Preheat air fryer to 190°C
2. Drizzle potatoes with oil, mix in salt and rosemary
3. Place in the air fryer and cook for 20 minutes turning halfway

Asparagus Fries

Servings: 2
Cooking Time:xx
Ingredients:

- 1 egg
- 1 tsp honey
- 100g panko bread crumbs
- Pinch of cayenne pepper
- 100g grated parmesan
- 12 asparagus spears
- 75g mustard
- 75g Greek yogurt

Directions:

1. Preheat air fryer to 200°C
2. Combine egg and honey in a bowl, mix panko crumbs and parmesan on a plate
3. Coat each asparagus in egg then in the bread crumbs
4. Place in the air fryer and cook for about 6 mins
5. Mix the remaining ingredients in a bowl and serve as a dipping sauce

Mediterranean Vegetables

Servings: 1–2
Cooking Time:xx
Ingredients:

- 1 courgette/zucchini, thickly sliced
- 1 (bell) pepper, deseeded and chopped into large chunks
- 1 red onion, sliced into wedges
- 12 cherry tomatoes
- 1 tablespoon olive oil
- ½ teaspoon salt
- ½ teaspoon freshly ground black pepper
- 2 rosemary twigs
- mozzarella, fresh pesto (see page 80) and basil leaves, to serve

Directions:

1. Preheat the air-fryer to 180°C/350°F.
2. Toss the prepared vegetables in the oil and seasoning. Add the vegetables and the rosemary to the preheated air-fryer and air-fry for 12–14 minutes, depending on how 'chargrilled' you like them.
3. Remove and serve topped with fresh mozzarella and pesto and scattered with basil leaves.

Onion Rings

Servings: 4
Cooking Time:xx
Ingredients:

- 200g flour
- 75g cornstarch
- 2 tsp baking powder
- 1 tsp salt
- 2 pinches of paprika
- 1 large onion, cut into rings
- 1 egg
- 1 cup milk
- 200g breadcrumbs
- 2 pinches garlic powder

Directions:

1. Stir flour, salt, starch and baking powder together in a bowl
2. Dip onion rings into the flour mix to coat
3. Whisk the egg and milk into the flour mix, dip in the onion rings
4. Dip the onion rings into the bread crumbs
5. Heat the air fryer to 200°C
6. Place the onion rings in the air fryer and cook for 2-3 minutes until golden brown
7. Sprinkle with paprika and garlic powder to serve

Garlic And Parsley Potatoes

Servings: 4
Cooking Time:xx
Ingredients:

- 500g baby potatoes, cut into quarters
- 1 tbsp oil
- 1 tsp salt
- ½ tsp garlic powder
- ½ tsp dried parsley

Directions:

1. Preheat air fryer to 175°C
2. Combine potatoes and oil in a bowl
3. Add remaining ingredients and mix
4. Add to the air fryer and cook for about 25 minutes until golden brown, turning halfway through

Egg Fried Rice

Servings:2
Cooking Time:15 Minutes
Ingredients:

- 400 g / 14 oz cooked white or brown rice
- 100 g / 3.5 oz fresh peas and sweetcorn
- 2 tbsp olive oil
- 2 eggs, scrambled

Directions:

1. Preheat the air fryer to 150 °C / 300 °F and line the bottom of the basket with parchment paper.
2. In a bowl, mix the cooked white or brown rice and the fresh peas and sweetcorn.
3. Pour in 2 tbsp olive oil and toss to coat evenly. Stir in the scrambled eggs.
4. Transfer the egg rice into the lined air fryer basket, close the lid, and cook for 15 minutes until the eggs are cooked and the rice is soft.
5. Serve as a side dish with some cooked meat or tofu.

Sweet And Sticky Parsnips And Carrots

Servings:2
Cooking Time:15 Minutes

Ingredients:

- 4 large carrots, peeled and chopped into long chunks
- 4 large parsnips, peeled and chopped into long chunks
- 1 tbsp olive oil
- 2 tbsp honey
- 1 tsp dried mixed herbs

Directions:

1. Preheat the air fryer to 150 °C / 300 °F and line the bottom of the basket with parchment paper.
2. Place the chopped carrots and parsnips in a large bowl and drizzle over the olive oil and honey. Sprinkle in some black pepper to taste and toss well to fully coat the vegetables.
3. Transfer the coated vegetables into the air fryer basket and shut the lid. Cook for 20 minutes until the carrots and parsnips and cooked and crispy.
4. Serve as a side with your dinner.

Super Easy Fries

Servings: 2
Cooking Time:xx

Ingredients:

- 500g potatoes cut into ½ inch sticks
- 1 tsp olive oil
- ¼ tsp salt
- ¼ tsp pepper

Directions:

1. Place the potatoes in a bowl cover with water and allow to soak for 30 minutes
2. Spread the butter onto one side of the bread slices
3. Pat dry with paper, drizzle with oil and toss to coat
4. Place in the air fryer and cook at 200°C for about 15 minutes, keep tossing through cooking time
5. Sprinkle with salt and pepper

Zingy Brussels Sprouts

Servings: 2
Cooking Time:xx
Ingredients:

- 1 tbsp avocado oil
- ½ tsp salt
- ½ tsp pepper
- 400g Brussels sprouts halved
- 1 tsp balsamic vinegar
- 2 tsp crumbled bacon

Directions:

1. Preheat air fryer to 175°C
2. Combine oil, salt and pepper in a bowl and mix well. Add Brussels sprouts
3. Place in the air fryer and cook for 5 minutes shake then cook for another 5 minutes
4. Sprinkle with balsamic vinegar and sprinkle with bacon

Hasselback New Potatoes

Servings: 4
Cooking Time:xx
Ingredients:

- 8–12 new potatoes, roughly 5–7 cm/2–2¾ in. in length
- 2 teaspoons olive oil
- salt
- 1 tablespoon butter (optional)

Directions:

1. Preheat the air-fryer to 180°C/350°F.
2. Slice the potatoes multiple times widthways, making sure you do not cut all the way through (if you place the potatoes in the bowl of a wooden spoon to make these slices, it prevents you cutting all the way through). Coat the potatoes in the olive oil and sprinkle over the salt.
3. Add the potatoes to the preheated air-fryer and air-fry for 20–25 minutes until the potatoes are crispy on the outside but soft on the inside. Serve immediately.

Yorkshire Puddings

Servings: 2
Cooking Time:xx

Ingredients:

- 1 tablespoon olive oil
- 70 g/½ cup plus ½ tablespoon plain/all-purpose flour (gluten-free if you wish)
- 100 ml/7 tablespoons milk
- 2 eggs
- salt and freshly ground black pepper

Directions:

1. You will need 4 ramekins. Preheat the air-fryer to 200°C/400°F.
2. Using a pastry brush, oil the base and sides of each ramekin, dividing the oil equally between the ramekins. Place the greased ramekins in the preheated air-fryer and heat for 5 minutes.
3. Meanwhile, in a food processor or using a whisk, combine the flour, milk, eggs and seasoning until you have a batter that is frothy on top. Divide the batter equally between the preheated ramekins. Return the ramekins to the air-fryer and air-fry for 20 minutes without opening the drawer. Remove the Yorkshire puddings from the ramekins and serve immediately.

Desserts Recipes

Brownies

Servings: 6
Cooking Time:xx

Ingredients:

- 25g melted butter
- 50g sugar
- 1 egg
- ½ tsp vanilla
- 25g flour
- 3 tbsp cocoa
- ⅛ tsp baking powder
- ⅛ tsp salt

Directions:

1. Preheat the air fryer to 165°C
2. Add all the wet ingredients to a bowl and combine.
3. Add the dry ingredients and mix well
4. Place the batter into a prepared pan and cook in the air fryer for 13 minutes

Chocolate And Berry Pop Tarts

Servings:8
Cooking Time:10 Minutes

Ingredients:

- For the filling:
- 50 g / 1.8 oz fresh raspberries
- 50 g / 1.8 oz fresh strawberries
- 100 g / 3.5 oz granulated sugar
- 1 tsp corn starch
- For the pastry:
- 1 sheet puff pastry
- For the frosting:
- 4 tbsp powdered sugar
- 2 tbsp maple syrup or honey
- Chocolate sprinkles

Directions:

1. Preheat the air fryer to 180 °C / 350 °F and line the mesh basket with parchment paper or grease it with olive oil.
2. Make the filling by combining the strawberries, raspberries, and granulated sugar in a saucepan. Place on medium heat until the mixture starts to boil. When it begins to boil, turn the temperature down to a low setting. Use a spoon to break up the berries and forms a smooth mixture.
3. Stir in the corn starch and let the mixture simmer for 1-2 minutes. Remove the saucepan from the heat and set aside to cool while you prepare the pastry.
4. Roll out the large sheet of puff pastry and cut it into 8 equal rectangles.
5. Spoon 2 tbsp of the cooled berry filling onto one side of each rectangle. Fold over the other side of each puff pastry rectangle to cover the filling. Press the sides down with a fork or using your fingers to seal the filling into the pastry.
6. Transfer the puff pastry rectangles into the lined air fryer basket. Cook for 10-12 minutes until the pastry is golden and crispy.
7. Meanwhile, make the frosting. Whisk together the powdered sugar, maple syrup or honey, and chocolate chips in a bowl until well combined.
8. Carefully spread a thin layer of frosting in the centre of each pop tart. Allow the frosting to set before serving.

White Chocolate Pudding

Servings:2
Cooking Time:15 Minutes
Ingredients:

- 100 g / 3.5 oz white chocolate
- 50 g brown sugar
- 2 tbsp olive oil
- ½ tsp vanilla extract
- 4 egg whites, plus two egg yolks

Directions:

1. Preheat the air fryer to 180 °C / 350 °F and line the mesh basket with parchment paper or grease it with olive oil.
2. Place the white chocolate in a saucepan and place it over low heat until it melts, being careful not to let the chocolate burn.
3. Stir in the brown sugar, olive oil, and vanilla extract.
4. Whisk the egg whites and egg yolks in a bowl until well combined. Fold a third of the eggs into the white chocolate mixture and stir until it forms a smooth and consistent mixture. Repeat twice more with the other two-thirds of the eggs.
5. Pour the white chocolate pudding mixture evenly into two ramekins and place the ramekins in the lined air fryer basket. Cook for 15 minutes until the pudding is hot and set on top.

Cinnamon Bites

Servings: 8
Cooking Time:xx
Ingredients:

- 200g flour
- 200g whole wheat flour
- 2 tbsp sugar
- 1 tsp baking powder
- ¼ tsp cinnamon
- 3 tbsp water
- ¼ tsp salt
- 4 tbsp butter
- 25ml milk
- Cooking spray
- 350g powdered sugar

Directions:

1. Mix together flour, sugar, baking powder and salt in a bowl
2. Add the butter and mix well
3. Add the milk and mix to form a dough
4. Knead until dough is smooth, cut into 16 pieces
5. Roll each piece into a small ball
6. Coat the air fryer with cooking spray and heat to 175°C
7. Add the balls to the air fryer and cook for 12 minutes
8. Mix the powdered sugar and water together, decorate

Chocolate Eclairs

Servings: 9
Cooking Time:xx

Ingredients:

- 100g plain flour
- 50g butter
- 3 eggs
- 150ml water
- 25g butter
- 1 tsp vanilla extract
- 1 tsp icing sugar
- 150ml whipped cream
- 50g milk chocolate
- 1 tbsp whipped cream

Directions:

1. Preheat the air fryer to 180ºC
2. Add 50g of butter to a pan along with the water and melt over a medium heat
3. Remove from the heat and stir in the flour. Return to the heat until mix form a single ball of dough
4. Allow to cool, once cool beat in the eggs until you have a smooth dough
5. Make into eclair shapes, cook in the air fryer at 180ºC for 10 minutes and then 160ºC for 8 minutes
6. Mix the vanilla, icing sugar and 150ml of whipping cream until nice and thick
7. Once cool fill each eclair with the cream mix
8. Place the chocolate, 1 tbsp whipped cream and 25g of butter in a glass bowl and melt over a pan of boiling water. Top the eclairs

Chocolate Souffle

Servings:2
Cooking Time:15 Minutes

Ingredients:

- 2 eggs
- 4 tbsp brown sugar
- 1 tsp vanilla extract
- 4 tbsp butter, melted
- 4 tbsp milk chocolate chips
- 4 tbsp flour

Directions:

1. Preheat the air fryer to 180 °C / 350 °F. Remove the mesh basket from the machine and line it with parchment paper.
2. Separate the egg whites from the egg yolks and place them in two separate bowls.
3. Beat the yolks together with the brown sugar, vanilla extract, melted butter, milk chocolate chips, and flour in a bowl. It should form a smooth, consistent mixture.
4. Whisk the egg whites until they form stiff peaks. In batches, fold the egg whites into the chocolate mixture.
5. Divide the batter evenly between two souffle dishes and place them in the lined air fryer basket.
6. Cook the souffle dishes for 15 minutes until hot and set.

Banana Bread

Servings: 8
Cooking Time:xx
Ingredients:

- 200g flour
- 1 tsp cinnamon
- ½ tsp salt
- ¼ tsp baking soda
- 2 ripe banana mashed
- 2 large eggs
- 75g sugar
- 25g plain yogurt
- 2 tbsp oil
- 1 tsp vanilla extract
- 2 tbsp chopped walnuts
- Cooking spray

Directions:

1. Line a 6 inch cake tin with parchment paper and coat with cooking spray
2. Whisk together flour, cinnamon, salt and baking soda set aside
3. In another bowl mix together remaining ingredients, add the flour mix and combine well
4. Pour batter into the cake tin and place in the air fryer
5. Cook at 155°C for 35 minutes turning halfway through

Cherry Pies

Servings: 6
Cooking Time:xx
Ingredients:

- 300g prepared shortcrust pastry
- 75g cherry pie filling
- Cooking spray
- 3 tbsp icing sugar
- ½ tsp milk

Directions:

1. Cut out 6 pies with a cookie cutter
2. Add 1 ½ tbsp filling to each pie
3. Fold the dough in half and seal around the edges with a fork
4. Place in the air fryer, spray with cooking spray
5. Cook at 175°C for 10 minutes
6. Mix icing sugar and milk and drizzled over cooled pies to serve

Apple Crumble

Servings: 4
Cooking Time:xx
Ingredients:

- 2 apples (each roughly 175 g/6 oz.), cored and chopped into 2-cm/¾-in cubes
- 3 tablespoons unrefined sugar
- 100 g/1 cup jumbo rolled oats/old-fashioned oats
- 40 g/heaped ¼ cup flour (gluten-free if you wish)
- 1 heaped teaspoon ground cinnamon
- 70 g/scant ⅓ cup cold butter, chopped into small cubes

Directions:

1. Preheat the air-fryer to 180°C/350°F.
2. Scatter the apple pieces in a baking dish that fits your air-fryer, then sprinkle over 1 tablespoon sugar. Add the baking dish to the preheated air-fryer and air-fry for 5 minutes.
3. Meanwhile, in a bowl mix together the oats, flour, remaining sugar and cold butter. Use your fingertips to bring the crumble topping together.
4. Remove the baking dish from the air-fryer and spoon the crumble topping over the partially cooked apple. Return the baking dish to the air dryer and air-fry for a further 10 minutes. Serve warm or cold.

Peach Pies(2)

Servings: 8
Cooking Time:xx
Ingredients:

- 2 peaches, peeled and chopped
- 1 tbsp lemon juice
- 3 tbsp sugar
- 1 tsp vanilla extract
- ¼ tsp salt
- 1 tsp cornstarch
- 1 pack ready made pastry
- Cooking spray

Directions:

1. Mix together peaches, lemon juice, sugar and vanilla in a bowl. Stand for 15 minutes
2. Drain the peaches keeping 1 tbsp of the liquid, mix cornstarch into the peaches
3. Cut the pastry into 8 circles, fill with the peach mix
4. Brush the edges of the pastry with water and fold over to form half moons, crimp the edges to seal
5. Coat with cooking spray
6. Add to the air fryer and cook at 170°C for 12 minutes until golden brown

Pop Tarts

Servings: 6
Cooking Time:xx

Ingredients:

- 200g strawberries quartered
- 25g sugar
- ½ pack ready made pie crust
- Cooking spray
- 50g powdered sugar
- 1 ½ tsp lemon juice
- 1 tbsp sprinkles

Directions:

1. Stir together strawberries and sugar in a bowl
2. Allow to stand for 15 minutes then microwave on high for 10 minutes stirring halfway through
3. Roll out pie crust into 12 inch circle, cut into 12 rectangles
4. Spoon mix onto 6 of the rectangles
5. Brush the edges with water and top with the remaining rectangles
6. Press around the edges with a fork to seal
7. Place in the air fryer and cook at 175°C for about 10 minutes
8. Mix together powdered sugar and decorate add sprinkles

Lemon Tarts

Servings: 8
Cooking Time:xx

Ingredients:

- 100g butter
- 225g plain flour
- 30g caster sugar
- Zest and juice of 1 lemon
- 4 tsp lemon curd

Directions:

1. In a bowl mix together butter, flour and sugar until it forms crumbs, add the lemon zest and juice
2. Add a little water at a time and mix to form a dough
3. Roll out the dough and line 8 small ramekins with it
4. Add ¼ tsp of lemon curd to each ramekin
5. Cook in the air fryer for 15 minutes at 180°C

Thai Fried Bananas

Servings: 8
Cooking Time:xx
Ingredients:

- 4 ripe bananas
- 2 tbsp flour
- 2 tbsp rice flour
- 2 tbsp cornflour
- 2 tbsp desiccated coconut
- Pinch salt
- ½ tsp baking powder
- ½ tsp cardamon powder

Directions:

1. Place all the dry ingredients in a bowl and mix well. Add a little water at a time and combine to form a batter
2. Cut the bananas in half and then half again length wise
3. Line the air fryer with parchment paper and spray with cooking spray
4. Dip each banana piece in the batter mix and place in the air fryer
5. Cook at 200°C for 10 -15 minutes turning halfway
6. Serve with ice cream

Peanut Butter & Chocolate Baked Oats

Servings:9
Cooking Time:xx
Ingredients:

- 150 g/1 heaped cup rolled oats/quick-cooking oats
- 50 g/⅓ cup dark chocolate chips or buttons
- 300 ml/1¼ cups milk or plant-based milk
- 50 g/3½ tablespoons Greek or plant-based yogurt
- 1 tablespoon runny honey or maple syrup
- ½ teaspoon ground cinnamon or ground ginger
- 65 g/scant ⅓ cup smooth peanut butter

Directions:

1. Stir all the ingredients together in a bowl, then transfer to a baking dish that fits your air-fryer drawer.
2. Preheat the air-fryer to 180°C/350°F.
3. Add the baking dish to the preheated air-fryer and air-fry for 10 minutes. Remove from the air-fryer and serve hot, cut into 9 squares.

Pumpkin Spiced Bread Pudding

Servings: 2
Cooking Time:xx
Ingredients:

- 175g heavy cream
- 500g pumpkin puree
- 30ml milk
- 25g sugar
- 1 large egg, plus one extra yolk
- ⅛ tsp salt
- ½ tsp pumpkin spice
- 500g cubed crusty bread
- 4 tbsp butter

Directions:

1. Place all of the ingredients apart from the bread and butter into a bowl and mix.
2. Add the bread and melted butter to the bowl and mix well
3. Heat the air fryer to 175°C
4. Pour the mix into a baking tin and cook in the air fryer for 35-40 minutes
5. Serve with maple cream

Apple Chips With Yogurt Dip

Servings: 4
Cooking Time:xx
Ingredients:

- 1 apple
- 1 tsp cinnamon
- 2 tsp oil
- Cooking spray
- 25g greek yogurt
- 1 tbsp almond butter
- 1 tsp honey

Directions:

1. Thinly slice the apple, place in a bowl and coat with cinnamon and oil
2. Coat the air fryer with cooking spray and add the apple slices
3. Cook the slices for 12 minutes at 180°C
4. Mix the butter, honey and yogurt together and serve with the apple slices as a dip

Chocolate Cake

Servings: 2
Cooking Time:xx
Ingredients:

- 3 eggs
- 75ml sour cream
- 225g flour
- 150g sugar
- 2 tsp vanilla extract
- 25g cocoa powder
- 1 tsp baking powder
- ½ tsp baking soda

Directions:

1. Preheat the air fryer to 160°C
2. Mix all the ingredients together in a bowl
3. Pour into a greased baking tin
4. Place into the air fryer and cook for 25 minutes
5. Allow to cool and ice with chocolate frosting

Peach Pies(1)

Servings: 8
Cooking Time:xx
Ingredients:

- 2 peaches, peeled and chopped
- 1 tbsp lemon juice
- 3 tbsp sugar
- 1 tsp vanilla extract
- ¼ tsp salt
- 1 tsp cornstarch
- 1 pack of shortcrust pastry

Directions:

1. Stir together peaches, lemon juice, sugar, vanilla and salt allow to stand for 15 minutes
2. Drain the peaches keeping 1 tbsp of the juice
3. Mix the liquid with the cornstarch and mix into the peaches
4. Cut out 8 4 inch circles from the pastry. Add 1 tbsp of peach mix to each piece of pastry
5. Fold the dough over to create half moons, crimp the edges with a fork to seal. Spray with cooking spray
6. Place in the air fryer and cook at 180°C for 12-14 minutes

Coffee, Chocolate Chip, And Banana Bread

Servings:8
Cooking Time:1 Hour 10 Minutes

Ingredients:

- 200 g / 7 oz plain flour
- 1 tsp baking powder
- 1 tsp ground cinnamon
- 1 tbsp ground coffee
- ½ tsp salt
- 2 ripe bananas, peeled
- 2 eggs, beaten
- 100 g / 3.5 oz granulated sugar
- 50 g / 3.5 oz brown sugar
- 100 g / 3.5 oz milk chocolate chips
- 4 tbsp milk
- 2 tbsp olive oil
- 1 tsp vanilla extract

Directions:

1. Preheat the air fryer to 150 °C / 300 °F and line a loaf tin with parchment paper.
2. In a large mixing bowl, combine the plain flour, baking powder, ground cinnamon, and salt.
3. Mash the ripe bananas in a separate bowl until there are no lumps. Whisk in the beaten eggs, followed by the granulated sugar, brown sugar, and milk chocolate chips until well combined.
4. Stir in the milk, olive oil, and vanilla extract before combining the dry and wet ingredients. Mix until combined into one smooth mixture.
5. Pour the batter into the prepared loaf tin and transfer into the air fryer basket. Cook for 30-40 minutes until the cake is set and golden on top. Insert a knife into the centre of the cake. It should come out dry when the cake is fully cooked.
6. Remove the loaf tin from the air fryer and set aside to cool on a drying rack. Once cooled, remove the cake from the loaf tin and cut into slices.
7. Enjoy the cake hot or cold.

Chocolate Orange Muffins

Servings: 12
Cooking Time:xx

Ingredients:

- 100g self raising flour
- 110g caster sugar
- 50g butter
- 20g cocoa powder
- 50ml milk
- 1 tsp cocoa nibs
- 1 large orange juice and rind
- 1 tbsp honey
- 1tsp vanilla essence
- 2 eggs

Directions:

1. Add the flour, butter and sugar to a mixing bowl and rug together
2. Add the cocoa, honey, orange and vanilla mix well
3. Mix the milk and egg together then add to the flour mix, combine well
4. Rub your muffin cases with flour to stop them sticking, add 2 tbsp batter to each one
5. Cook in the air fryer for 12 minutes at 180°C

Chocolate Shortbread Balls

Servings: 9
Cooking Time:13 Minutes

Ingredients:

- 175g butter
- 75g caster sugar
- 250g plain flour
- 2 tsp vanilla essence
- 9 chocolate chunks
- 2 tbsp cocoa powder

Directions:

1. Preheat the air fryer to 180°C
2. Add the flour, sugar and cocoa to a bowl and mix well
3. Rub in the butter and vanilla then knead into a smooth dough
4. Divide the mix into 9, place a chunk of chocolate in each piece and form into balls covering the chocolate
5. Place the balls in the air fryer and cook at 180°C for 8 mins then a further 6 mins at 160°C

Sweet Potato Dessert Fries

Servings: 4
Cooking Time:xx

Ingredients:

- 2 sweet potatoes, peeled
- ½ tbsp coconut
- 1 tbsp arrowroot
- 2 tsp melted butter
- ½ cup coconut sugar
- 2 tsp cinnamon
- Icing sugar

Directions:

1. Cut the potatoes into ½ inch thick strips, coat in arrowroot and coconut oil
2. Place in the air fryer and cook at 190°C for 18 minutes shaking halfway through
3. Remove from air fryer and place in a bowl, drizzle with melted butter
4. Mix in sugar and cinnamon
5. Sprinkle with icing sugar to serve

RECIPES INDEX

A

Air Fried Maple Chicken Thighs 70

Air Fryer Bbq Chicken 75

Air Fryer Cheese Sandwich 25

Alternative Stuffed Potatoes 83

Apple Chips With Yogurt Dip 97

Apple Crisps 21

Apple Crumble 94

Asian Meatballs 56

Asparagus Fries 84

Asparagus Spears 83

Aubergine Parmesan 82

B

Baba Ganoush 21

Bacon Smokies 33

Baked Aubergine Slices With Yogurt Dressing 23

Baked Panko Cod 49

Banana Bread 93

Bbq Chicken Tenders 66

Bbq Soy Curls 29

Beef Bulgogi Burgers 66

Beef Kebobs 56

Blanket Breakfast Eggs 13

Breakfast "pop Tarts" 20

Breakfast Doughnuts 17

Broccoli Cheese 23

Brownies 89

Buffalo Wings 77

Buttermilk Chicken 77

Butternut Squash 78

Butternut Squash Falafel 27

C

Cauliflower With Hot Sauce And Blue Cheese Sauce 81

Char Siu Buffalo 64

Charred Chicken Breasts 69

Cheddar & Bbq Stuffed Chicken 76

Cheese Scones 19

Cheese Wontons 43

Cheese, Tomato & Pesto Crustless Quiches 31

Cherry Pies 93

Chicken & Bacon Parcels 36

Chicken And Cheese Chimichangas 72

Chicken Fajitas 74

Chicken Fried Rice 67

Chicken Parmesan With Marinara Sauce 76

Chicken Tikka 68

Chinese Chilli Beef 65

Chinese Pork With Pineapple 63

Chocolate And Berry Pop Tarts 90

Chocolate Cake 98

Chocolate Eclairs 92

Chocolate Orange Muffins 100

Chocolate Shortbread Balls 100

Chocolate Souffle 92

Cinnamon Bites 91

Coconut Shrimp 44

Coffee, Chocolate Chip, And Banana Bread 99

Corn Nuts 41

Courgette Fries 18

Courgette Gratin 81

Courgette Meatballs 32

Crispy Broccoli 80

Crispy Nacho Prawns 48

Crunchy Fish 47

Cumin Shoestring Carrots 14

E

Easy Air Fryer Sausage 17

Easy Cheesy Scrambled Eggs 16

Egg Fried Rice 86

F

Fillet Mignon Wrapped In Bacon 59

Fish In Parchment Paper 48

Fish Sticks With Tartar Sauce Batter 47

Fish Taco Cauliflower Rice Bowls 45

French Toast 13

G

Garlic And Parsley Potatoes 86

Garlic Cheese Bread 33

Garlic Pizza Toast 36

Garlic-parsley Prawns 51

Gluten Free Honey And Garlic Shrimp 50

Gnocchi Caprese 30

Goat's Cheese Tartlets 25

Grain-free Chicken Katsu 71

H

Halloumi Fries 11

Hamburgers With Feta 59

Hard Boiled Eggs Air Fryer Style 18

Hasselback New Potatoes 88

Hawaiian Chicken 75

Healthy Bang Bang Chicken 69

Healthy Breakfast Bagels 20

Healthy Stuffed Peppers 12

Homemade Croquettes 79

Honey Cajun Chicken Thighs 67

I

Italian Rice Balls 42

J

Jalapeño Poppers 37

Japanese Pork Chops 58

K

Korean Chicken Wings 34

L

Lamb Calzone 58

Lemon Pepper Shrimp 55

Lemon Tarts 95

M

Mac & Cheese Bites 39

Mahi Fish Tacos 53

Meatballs In Tomato Sauce 61

Mediterranean Vegetables 85

Mini Quiche 26

Miso Mushrooms On Sourdough Toast 30

Mongolian Beef 55

Mozzarella Sticks 37

O

Olive Stained Turkey Breast 74

Onion Bahji 40

Onion Pakoda 35

Onion Rings 85

Oozing Baked Eggs 19

Orange Sesame Cauliflower 80

P

Parmesan-coated Fish Fingers 49

Patatas Bravas 11

Peach Pies(1) 98

Peach Pies(2) 94

Peanut Butter & Chocolate Baked Oats 96

Pepperoni Bread 39

Peppery Lemon Shrimp 54

Pesto Salmon 44

Pizza Chicken Nuggets 78

Plantain Fries 12

Pop Tarts 95

Popcorn Tofu 41

Pork Belly With Crackling 62

Pork Chilli Cheese Dogs 65

Pork Chops With Raspberry And Balsamic 64

Potato Fries 15

Potato Wedges With Rosemary 84

Pretzel Bites 35

Pumpkin Spiced Bread Pudding 97

Q

Quick Chicken Nuggets 73

Quinoa-stuffed Romano Peppers 24

R

Raspberry Breakfast Pockets 15

Ravioli Air Fryer Style 28

Roast Pork 63

Roasted Okra 82

S

Salt And Pepper Belly Pork 57

Salt And Vinegar Chips 38

Sausage Burritos 60

Scotch Eggs 43

Shakshuka 29

Shrimp With Yum Yum Sauce 46

Shrimp Wrapped With Bacon 46

Spicy Peanuts 42

Spinach And Feta Croissants 26

Steak And Mushrooms 62

Sticky Tofu With Cauliflower Rice 27

Store-cupboard Fishcakes 51

Super Easy Fries 87

Sweet And Sticky Parsnips And Carrots 87

Sweet Potato Dessert Fries 101

Sweet Potato Taquitos 28

T

Taco Lasagne Pie 61

Tahini Beef Bites 60

Tandoori Salmon 50

Tangy Breakfast Hash 14

Tasty Pumpkin Seeds 38

Tempura Veggies 32

Tex Mex Hash Browns 79

Thai Fried Bananas 96

Thai Salmon Patties 54

Thai Turkey Burgers 73

Thai-style Tuna Fishcakes 52

Tilapia Fillets 45

Tofu Bowls 31

Tortellini Bites 40

Traditional Empanadas 57

Traditional Fish And Chips 53

Turkey Cutlets In Mushroom Sauce 72

V

Veggie Bakes 22

Veggie Lasagne 22

W

Waffle Fries 34

White Chocolate Pudding 91

Whole Chicken 68

Whole Wheat Pizza 24

Y

Yorkshire Puddings 89

Your Favourite Breakfast Bacon 16

Z

Zingy Brussels Sprouts 88

Printed in Great Britain
by Amazon

35297967R00059